Toxicity: Avoid It; Eliminate It

Dr. Jason Pfledderer

Cover design by: K&T Graphics

Edited by: Critique Editing Services, LLC

Acknowledgements

I'd like to first thank the Holy Spirit for even speaking to me. Then God the Father for sending His Son Jesus Christ to pay the penalty for my sins and not giving me the punishment that I rightfully deserve.

Then to my loving wife Yankho for taking care of all of those household duties while I plugged away on yet another project.

Then to my lifelong friend C.L. for helping me put my ideas into a usable format, then taking my projects to the next level.

To Dr. Mark Lantz for his mentorship, his study notes (which were used with permission) and his daily encouragement.

To Professor Roger Krynock for keeping me theologically correct.

To Karen and Jen for finally making sure it all "flows" without a hitch.

And then to Natasha for taking my vision and transforming it into picture form.

For without all of you this, and many other projects, wouldn't be possible. May God bless you all.

Table of Contents

A cardinal rule of Biblical interpretation, as in the case of the interpretation of any written document, is always **"context rules."**

My job as a Biblical expositor is always to determine the meaning that the original Biblical author—and ultimately God Himself—intended a passage to mean. Therefore, I would like to make this disclaimer:

With the vast array of denominations and the large numbers of theologians, there are a myriad of opinions on Biblical topics. Knowing this, I have made every effort to line up the contents of this book as closely as possible with Scripture.

Introduction

And, behold, there was a woman which had a spirit of infirmity eighteen years, and was bowed together, and could in no wise lift up herself. (Luke 13:11)

There are some people who are so bound in life by toxic spirits and toxic people that all they can do is look down. The woman in this text could not lift herself up because of the spirit of infirmity that had her bound for eighteen years. Think about that . . . for eighteen years the only thing she could see was the ground. The only direction she could look in was down. She couldn't look up and see the beauty of the world around her because she was bound. She couldn't lift up her head and engage in healthy conversation with others because of a spirit of infirmity. What a miserable life it was for this poor woman. Eighteen years of looking down . . . until she met Jesus. When she met Him, *"he laid [his] hands on her: and immediately she was made straight, and glorified God"* (Luke 13:13).

There are many people like this woman, maybe not physically, but spiritually and emotionally. All they can do is look down in life. They don't see anything positive about living. They complain about everything. They don't see the beauty in the world around them. They cannot engage in healthy conversation with anyone because they look down on themselves and on everyone around them. Maybe this is you. Do you complain about everything and can't seem to find anything positive to think or talk about?

1

If so, my friend, then you are bound. Today is the day you need to come to Jesus and allow Him to *"straighten you up"*—straighten up your perspective of yourself and life, allow His touch to detoxify you, and cause you to stand tall again to see things you have never seen, to be the person you were created to be, for both you and the people around you.

Today is a new day for you! It's time for you to be healed from looking down, so you can look up and see who Jesus is and who you are in Him. Let the Lord show you what a toxin-free life both looks and feels like. Be blessed today and look up!

Understand that when I refer to toxins, I am not just talking about substances such as drugs and alcohol. Yes, those are indeed toxic substances that you must avoid in order to have a God-driven purposeful existence. But along with that substance-free life, you must also limit your exposure to toxic relationshipsm and be able to correctly handle the toxic things and people of this world appropriately or outright learn how to avoid them.

This world is full of toxicity. Every single day we are bombarded by toxic people. Many of us have toxic relationships in our lives: those who live with a victim mentality or are possessed by evil spirits. How we deal with those people and those spirits will directly affect who we are, who we become, and how God uses us.

There are many spirits offending us at every turn. We here in America live in a nation of offended people. We are offended by everything. This book will help you set boundaries with toxic people and teach you how to not only avoid offending spirits but also set boundaries to protect yourself from them.

By the end of this book, you will gain knowledge about toxic people and toxic spirits and will possess a strategy that will not only help you live a better life but also help you to help others live a toxic-free life. All of it will be based on God's teachings.

CHAPTER 2

The New Clean You

And you shall love the Lord your God with all your heart and with all your soul and with all your mind and with all your strength. The second is this: "You shall love your neighbor as yourself." There is no other commandment greater than these. (Mark 12:30-31 ESV)

Isn't this so much easier said than done? Two things bear comment:

#1. Jesus used the Greek verb for love, ἀγαπάω. It is not a word having to do with emotion. It is a word that means love of the will, which is why Jesus could tell his followers to love their enemies. Biblical love is not motivated by emotion; rather, it is an act of the will, choosing to do another person good. Here, Jesus exhorted his followers to choose to do their neighbor—whoever that might be—good.

#2. When Jesus said, "as yourself," his words are an ellipsis. Filling in the ellipsis, this statement of Jesus reads: "love your neighbor as [you already love] yourself."

What Jesus means is that you already choose—as an act of your will—to make choices for your own good. Jesus was exhorting his followers to treat others the same way that they already treated themselves.

"Like" is another matter altogether. I should not "like" my actions when they are not in keeping with God's moral law—if I lie, cheat, steal, slander, or a hundred other actions. I should not "like" myself for doing those things. They violate my own conscience. It is hard to like myself at times—and sometimes, *it should be!*

After all, it's hard enough to even like ourselves half of the time. Love for ourselves and others oftentimes is a notion we want to incorporate into our lives, but simply cannot manage it. Then we find ourselves asking why. Could it be that we don't know how to get past our own hang-ups? Are we often critical of others because we see them portraying the same unhealthy traits we carry out in ourselves each day? Do we act in ways that cause us to dislike ourselves because of it? Are we the most toxic aspect of our own lives? The answer many times is—yes.

The key to getting along with others and avoiding toxicity in our lives is to first get along with ourselves.

Let me ask you this question: Do you believe God wants you to love other people? Of course you do . . . all of us do because we know Jesus commanded us to. But we forget that sandwiched in Jesus' command to love others is to also *"love thy neighbor as thyself."* Why did Jesus teach us that command? I believe it's because if we can't love ourselves first, then we won't truly love others effectively. I'm talking about true acceptance of who we are in Christ. We must accept the truths about what God has done *for us in Christ.*

He has made us his children—*(John 1:12)*

He has chosen us— *(Eph. 1:11)*

He has predestined us—*(Eph. 1:11)*

He has adopted us into his forever family as sons—*(Eph. 1:5)*

THE NEW CLEAN YOU

I have found that most people who are challenged in their relationships with others are struggling with who God has made them to be. My friend, today is the day to let that go. Learn to rejoice and be thankful for who you are in Christ. We must walk in the love and freedom He brings. When we learn to do that, I believe our acceptance of God's grace and love for us will heal our hearts, causing toxic moments to thrive no more. It begins with accepting God's love for us to be able to show love to others.

A reality we each must face is that we live in a world full of people, about seven billion. This is an amazing fact. What should not be so shocking to most of you is to learn that a great number of these people are toxic to our lives. This means that there are people who will bring about a harmful effect in our lives in either a subtle or not-so-subtle manner.

When I say toxic people, I think each of us have our own definition of what that may look like. To you, it may be a person who tries to intimidate and manipulate. For me, it's the kind of person who constantly contradicts and opposes everything I stand for. Toxicity is even more of a hindrance when it affects our spiritual and emotional health. For this reason—and more—we need to address toxic people.

While our definition of toxic people may differ, the principles of dealing with toxic people are grounded within the Word of God. Let's face it, we will be dealing with all manner of people for the rest of our lives, and the Lord yearns for us to deal with ourselves and others in a healthy manner.

> *Wherefore, my beloved, as ye have always obeyed, not as in my presence only, but now much more in my absence, work out your own salvation with fear and trembling. For it is God which worketh in you both to will and to do of his good pleasure. (Phil. 2:12-13)*

6

We don't have to sabotage our lives with toxic people. Even more, we must be sure that we are not the most toxic person in our lives. Beginning my study on this topic, I was amazed at how many Scriptures there were describing the power and importance of human relationships within our lives.

> Do not be misled: "Bad company corrupts good character."
> (1 Cor. 15:33 NIV)

> He that walketh with wise men shall be wise: but a companion of fools shall be destroyed. (Prov. 13:20)

Saying that we must all learn how to deal with toxic people seems like a no-brainer after reading such Scripture. What might not be so evident is when dealing with toxic people, we should begin first with ourselves. Yes, we might be the most toxic entity prohibiting our Godly growth. If we can learn to deal with our own toxicity, surely we can learn to deal with everyone else's in the most effective way.

Let's begin with how to deal with the most toxic person you will ever have to deal with—yourself. If you can learn to deal with your own toxicity, you'll be able to learn to deal with almost anyone else's.

Many of us can acknowledge the fact that relationally challenged people are generally those having the most difficult times dealing with themselves. This is true because oftentimes the way we see others is simply a reflection of how we are viewing ourselves inwardly. Regrettably, that toxicity carries over into our relationship with God. Let's use the Apostle Paul for an example, since he knew that he was his own worst enemy.

> I do not understand what I do. For what I want to do I do not do, but what I hate I do . . . For I do not do the good I want to do, but the evil I do not want to do—this I keep on doing. (Rom. 7:15, 19 NIV)

Therefore I do not run like someone running aimlessly; I do not fight like a boxer beating the air. No, I strike a blow to my body and make it my slave so that after I have preached to others, I myself will not be disqualified for the prize. (1 Cor. 9:26-27 NIV)

Can you relate to what Paul wrote? Don't you know the difference between acknowledging what is just and right versus actually doing what is right? Knowing how we are supposed to act but not doing so because it's too hard comes back to the old adage: it's easier said than done.

Paul had a built-in excuse. He could have blamed the Romans for the hardships in his life. He could have blamed the Pharisees. *Shoot!* He could have even blamed his fellow Jews. Yet he did not. He had the revelation that he was the most toxic person in his own life. *I know what I want to do. I know what I should do. But for some reason I keep doing what I'm not supposed to do!*

This is one great self-actualization. Paul understood that his greatest enemy was his own flesh. It was his own way of thinking. His own attitudes and perspectives toward life were creating his greatest problems.

How would the other Biblical characters have fared if they'd had such a revelation? Imagine the change that would've occurred in Egypt had the Pharaoh realized his own toxic nature when dealing with Moses. Would Pontius Pilate have changed Jesus' path if the governor had learned to confront his own toxic behaviors? Probably. These examples were not the great plan of God and had to occur the way they did, but you can still see how dealing with ourselves first could change so much.

Confronting ourselves inwardly is the key element to an external change. The Lord wants us to be changed. It's why there's so much Scripture referencing how we are made into a different person when we take on Christ. The "old us" dies and a new person is made.

I am crucified with Christ: nevertheless I live; yet not I, but Christ liveth in me: and the life which I now live in the flesh I live by the faith of the Son of God, who loved me, and gave himself for me. (Gal. 2:20)

As carnally minded people, we are living in sin. Once changed by the resurrection power of Christ, we are reborn spiritually. Still, we must learn to be remade emotionally and physically, stripping away toxins from our lives. Put plainly, oftentimes we are our own worst enemy. It's our own thinking, our own attitudes, our own perspectives toward life and others that cause us the most trouble. Before delving into worrying about how others affect us, we must first deal with ourselves. Usually what we find as a problem in others is, in fact, a character issue within ourselves. We, therefore, must detoxify ourselves before dealing with outside influences. Here are three objectives in healing from within.

Objective #1: We have to learn to be honest with ourselves.

Have you ever known people who lie so much that they believe their own lies? They tell those same lies over and over until they completely convince themselves that what they say really happened. It's hard to process as a person when the narrative is not the truth. We have to be honest with ourselves.

More often than not, the way we see others is a reflection of how we see ourselves. What we don't like about other people and their habits is usually the actions we exhibit and dislike about ourselves. For example, if I were to lie habitually, then I would not believe others or feel that I could trust them because I can't or don't fully even trust myself; therefore, this naturally will create a toxic relationship with another person or people.

A pet peeve of mine is unclear communication. It irritates me when I'm speaking to others and they mumble back or are distracted by something else around them when we are in discussion. I initially saw this as a character flaw in others who showed lack of focus and a notion of disrespect.

Upon introspection, I reasoned why this upset me so much. It went back to my adolescence and how I used to have a speech impediment that caused my words to run together. The embarrassment of it then still affected my responses. Once I realized this truth and recalled how upset that insecurity made me, a newfound sense of empathy for those I speak with emerged. I've learned to desire patience and look to help others in our communication, all because I was honest with myself and my own faults then and now. Self-reflection and self-understanding are paramount to healthy relationships in general.

We can much better understand ourselves after examining our relationships with others. I want you to begin this path to self-transformation by writing down ten habits or traits that you like about yourself.

_____

_____

_____

_____

_____

_____

_____

_____

Now I want you to write down ten habits or traits that bother you about other people. The reason for doing this quick task is a step in self-actualization.

_____

_____

_____

_____

_____

_____

_____

_____

_____

_____

Keep these two lists close to you. Read them at least once each morning. I want you to commit the information to memory. Why? Because the more that you are aware of what helps/hinders you, the more change that you can accept. Usually the traits that we care little for or that outright bother us in others are the same traits we dislike about ourselves. What many of us will learn through this process is that we criticize the same traits we exhibit. This truth takes me immediately to the parable of the speck and the beam.

> Why do you look at the speck of sawdust in your brother's eye and pay no attention to the plank in your own eye? How can you say to your brother, "Let me take the speck out of your eye," when all the time there is a plank in your own eye? (Matt. 7:3-4 NIV)

THE NEW CLEAN YOU

Our Savior teaches us the valuable lesson that often what we see as a shortcoming in others is magnified so much more in our own lives. Let's make this more personal. Think about your list of dislikes. Can you be honest with yourself and say that you display some of those traits? For example, you may have a difficult time trusting people because you have not dealt with a previous abandonment issue. It won't allow you to trust others, and seeing that in others upsets you. Or maybe you are the kind of person who has a constant need to prove to others that you are "always right." Deep down inside you may feel the insecurity of feeling unintelligent because when you were younger the other kids called you stupid. Ten, twenty or thirty years later, it might still affect you to the point where you're upset by know-it-alls.

Then again, you may dislike controlling individuals. You may have developed bossy tendencies that you don't particularly care for, and you can recognize that trait in others but not in yourself. Despite any characteristic, trait, or belief you may delineate, there's good news. Jesus Christ came to heal you from any and all characteristics you don't like about yourself. The Bible never lies, and it states,

> *Therefore if any man be in Christ, he is a new creature: old things are passed away; behold, all things are become new. (2 Cor. 5:17)*

Simple! There's your answer. He who is of Christ is remade with all the old, bad stuff falling away. The greatest part is God wants those toxins to go away more than you do. Jesus comes to us so that we can have renewed hope and a new perspective of ourselves. He helps change our minds, and the first step to dealing with toxicity in other people will be to deal with the toxicity within ourselves. We must examine ourselves first (1 Cor. 11:28). Then, we can remove the plank from our own eye. After that, we will see clearly the speck in our brother's eye.

Objective #2: We can learn to get along with ourselves.

What happens when we actually learn to look inwardly at ourselves—when we really take a sincere appraisal of our thoughts, actions, and intentions? When we make the appropriate changes, such as believing how much we are loved and accepted by the Lord, we begin loving others as we should. Doing so means doing something about the toxic behavior that we don't like about ourselves first. Once we have taken that task on, we are enabled to face the fear of changing ourselves. That change enables us to once again like our actions and therefore, ourselves. The key to getting along with others is to first get along with ourselves. So let's do that right now. I'd like for you to write down the ten most common thoughts that keep recurring in your mind throughout the day:

_____

_____

_____

_____

_____

_____

_____

_____

_____

_____

THE NEW CLEAN YOU

Write down your ten most common intentions:

_____

_____

_____

_____

_____

_____

_____

_____

_____

_____

Write down ten of your most repeated actions/habits throughout the day:

_____

_____

_____

_____

_____

_____

_____

_____

_____

_____

THE NEW CLEAN YOU

This exercise is to simply bring awareness to that fact that what we think about the most doesn't always line up perfectly with our intentions, thus resulting in actions. If we can start to change what we constantly are thinking about, we will change the toxic characteristics that we want to change within ourselves. Next, write down ten toxic characteristics that you'd like to change about yourself:

_____

_____

_____

_____

_____

_____

_____

_____

_____

_____

Now that you are aware of what needs to be changed within yourself, one by one you can start making the necessary adjustments to reach your full God-given potential.

> *And thou shalt love the Lord thy God with all thy heart, and with all thy soul, and with all thy mind, and with all thy strength: this is the first commandment. And the second is like, namely this, Thou shalt love thy neighbour as thyself. There is none other commandment greater than these. (Mark 12:30-31 NIV)*

THE NEW CLEAN YOU

Too often lost in this message that you *"shalt love your neighbor as thyself"* is the statement that God is telling *you* to love *yourself!* So if you can't love yourself, then you'll not know how to properly love another. Love is key. The Lord says love Me; love others. For true love to happen, you must truly accept who you are in Christ.

Remember, Paul repeats Jesus' thought in Ephesians 5:29, "After all, **no one ever hated their own body, but they feed and care for their body . . . .**" Where did Paul get this idea that no one (that means NO human being) ever (that means at any time) hates himself (the opposite of loving himself)? Answer, from Jesus, who affirmed that every human being loves himself and feeds and cares for himself.

We always make choices that we consider good for ourselves.

Even when a person chooses to commit suicide, he is doing what he feels is the best option for himself at that time. Life has become so hard that he believes the best thing he can do for himself is to end the pain—and that means taking his life.

Do you see that everyone already does this?

The issue is that we often do not **like** ourselves because we fail to obey the moral law of God; therefore, we feel shame and guilt. The Bible says that we should not like ourselves when we sin; we need to repent and do what is right. Then we will feel good about ourselves because our actions are righteous ones.

Learning to get along with yourself through the new life given to you by salvation in Christ means that you must think of yourself as a brand-new creature. This means that the attitude you carry about yourself is new. It also means dragging old unhealthy baggage into your new life is not something to be done. When we drag the things that were not productive in the past into our new life, all we are doing is dirtying up our new clean vessel that is our new life. Doing anything other than this is a disrespect to the new you. Let's do that now. Write down ten bad traits that you had before coming to Christ, and next to it write down what new Christ-like characteristic you have replaced it with (or need to replace it with):

Old   New

_____   _____

_____   _____

_____   _____

_____   _____

_____   _____

_____   _____

_____   _____

_____   _____

_____   _____

I can't tell you how disheartening it is to see a new child of God start toting their old bad habits into their new life. Too often the problems I continually see involve so many "believers" continuing to drag along their old baggage of beliefs even though they claim to be born again.

If your desire is to cleanse yourself of toxins, then you really have to learn what it means to be "reborn." Reborn means that what happened in the past really doesn't matter. Reborn to Christ means that you don't need the approval of those around you to make you better. The upgrade is performed. You need only to maintain that upgrade. Maintaining this work means pleasing God first and you second.

> *But God forbid that I should glory, save in the cross of our Lord Jesus Christ, by whom the world is crucified unto me, and I unto the world. For in Christ Jesus neither circumcision availeth anything, nor uncircumcision, but a new creature. (Gal. 6:14-15)*

After an experience at the cross, God sees us as perfect! In Biblical terminology the word *perfection* means *completeness*. In other words, there's nothing more that can be added to make us more complete. Paul wrote these words to tell us that there is nothing this world can do to validate us or make us who we are. We are not dependent upon this world to make us who we are or who we are not. His perfect work is done, concluded, over.

There are so many people in this world looking to other people to validate them or make them feel good about themselves. They are trying to fit into this world so they can be accepted and made to feel as if they're a part of something. When we come to the cross, however, the truth is that we already have all there is to gain. Nothing else is needed. We need only to recognize this truth and love God and others as we already love ourselves. We need to move forward to live a toxin-free life. We must relish in our completeness in Christ.

Sadly, too many people look in the mirror and envision all the old dirt that clung to them prior to their rebirth. All they can see is themselves as a dirty glass of water. They see the people they were before they were born again. This causes them to revisit that person who displayed the traits/actions who made them dislike themselves. It's so counterproductive. If this is you, ask yourself this question: Do you believe that God loves you? If you are a born-again Christian, then you should already know the answer. Yes, of course He does. God is the Father of love. He so loved us that He sacrificed His only Son for us to have eternal life *(John 3:16).*

To rid yourself of your own toxins means you have to make the decision to actually do something about those toxins. Otherwise, you'll be infested by toxic behavior your entire life.

Some people feel they don't deserve love. To that I point out Paul's words in the book of Romans, *"And hope does not put us to shame, because God's love has been poured out into our hearts through the Holy Spirit, who has been given to us" (Romans 5:5 NIV).* When I looked up the word "ashamed," I found this word: *kataischynō,* which means to blush with shame; to dishonor or disgrace.

There are so many people living every day ashamed of who they are. They blush with shame when they think about their past actions or even current thoughts. They are ashamed of their physical appearance or emotional makeup or scars. But if the love of God is shed abroad, poured into our hearts, there is no reason for us to be ashamed any longer.

We are loved by the Most High God. So if God loves us, we should believe what He has said about us. To do anything contrary would be like telling God that He's wrong. We are not a mistake. Knowing this, we need to make a resolution. Today we must begin fully understanding and believing that we are God's great children! Our baggage from our trip called life has been lost, and we have started over with all brand-new things. Our mindset, personality, character—everything is made perfect in Christ, and we can start this new life children of God, forgiven, and accepted by the Father. We can definitely enjoy the new us moving forward.

Objective #3: We must learn how to cleanse ourselves.

I want to give you a visual example of how we are made new through the salvation process. Take a clear drinking glass from your cabinet at home. Fill that glass with water almost to the top. Now take a bottle of food coloring and drop a few drops of the coloring into the glass of clear water. Before your salvation, that polluted glass of water is you.

When you put your faith in Christ, you are made into a brand new glass of pure, clean water. After salvation you take that glass of dirty water and you dump it out. Then you take that dish soap and thoroughly wash that glass clean, which is you.

Now fill that clean glass back up with purified water. After doing so, you are made into a fresh, perfectly clean and refreshing substance, something worthy of being called new and pure. That's how the Lord sees you. The problem is that life simply keeps happening. Time often will pollute that clear, clean glass of water again. If left to sit there, eventually dust and other pollutants will come and slowly make the water unclean again.

Now take a drop of that food coloring and drop it into that fresh glass of water—this represents sin. Sin is inevitable. We cannot remain perfect. We are not able to stay pure. This is why we need the Lord Jesus Christ and His Holy Spirit in our lives. Through a constant and loving relationship with Him we can be purified each day. We die to ourselves a little more each day. What this does is allows the Son's Spirit to slowly purge our sin. Through His work, that daily junk is cleansed away making us clean again.

Take a large pitcher of water and pour it into the glass. As the clean water goes in and overflows the glass, the escaping water takes with it all the dirt (sin), making the water pure again. We are left with a pure, clean vessel.

This is our example of how we are to live our life—John tells us in 1 John 1:9 that *"If we confess our sins, **he is faithful and just and will forgive us our sins and purify us from all unrighteousness"** (NIV; emphasis added).* It is therefore God who does the work of forgiving and cleansing everyone.

So let's do that right now. Let's pray and ask God the Father if there are any sins that we need to be cleansed of:

_____

_____

_____

_____

_____

_____

_____

_____

_____

_____

Okay. We began living our new life in Christ with our brand-new body, soul, and outlook. However, just like buying a brand-new car, we managed to get a little dirt on it. Life is going to get us dirty. We have all sinned despite our best efforts. God knows we will not stay clean. He knows it's a function beyond our reach. But it's what we do after we get dirty that matters the most.

We have all heard of the physical cleanse or detox that people do. Why do you think they do that? It's to rid the body of toxins brought into their bodies by what they eat or drink. Those toxins have caused the body to feel unhealthy or weak. To expel that, a person goes through the cleansing process.

While there is definitive value in the body cleanse for your physical health, there's an even greater value in a cleanse for your spiritual health. Trichotomy is the belief that man is tripartite: body, soul, and spirit. As God is a tripartite—Father, Son, and Holy Spirit— so man is three parts—body, soul and spirit. This belief of explicit divisions, the Apostle Paul writes in 1 Thessalonians 5:23, *"And the very God of peace sanctify you wholly; and I pray God your whole **spirit** and **soul** and **body** be preserved blameless unto the coming of our Lord Jesus Christ"* (emphasis added).

However, many contemporary theologians would argue against this position. Their argument is that a person's "soul" involves his intellect, emotion, and will as distinct from the "spirit," which is then viewed as the higher faculty in a person that cannot be defended Biblically. They say that the Bible clearly teaches that man is a unified being—body and spirit. This unity is divisible into two aspects just mentioned, material (body) and immaterial (spirit). In the Bible these aspects—material and immaterial—are variously termed:

body (Greek: σῶμα) and soul (Greek: ψυχή) —*(Matt. 10:28)*

body (Greek: σῶμα) and mind (Greek: νοὸς)—*(Rom. 12:1-2)*

body (Greek: σῶμα) and spirit (Greek: πνεῦμα) —*(1 Cor. 7:34 or James 2:26)*

flesh (Greek: σάρξ) and spirit (Greek: πνεῦμά) —*(1 Cor. 5:5; 2 Cor. 7:1)*

flesh (Greek: σάρξ) and heart (Greek: καρδία) —*(Rom. 2:28-29)*

Other terms are also used: *"Love the Lord your God with all your heart* (Greek: καρδία) *and with all your soul* (Greek: ψυχή), *and with all your mind* (διάνοια)" *(Matt. 22.37; emphasis added).*

However, Mark reads this way: *"Love the Lord your God with all your heart* (Greek: καρδία) *and with all your soul* (Greek: ψυχή), *and with all your mind* (Greek: διάνοια), *and with all your strength* (Greek: ἰσχύος)" *(Mark 12.30; emphasis added).*

If we consider these quotations of Jesus' words, we would believe that man is not a tripartite being. If the mere enumeration of synonyms indicates *separate parts* of the material and immaterial nature of a human being, then we would be forced to the conclusion that the following list of Jesus' terms would lead to man's being a six-part being:

Heart — καρδία

Soul — ψυχή

Mind — διάνοια or νοὸς

Spirit — πνεῦμα

Strength — ἰσχύος

[Adding the material part] Body — σῶμα

Jesus was clearly piling up synonymous terms to make a powerful point: Love God with your *entire being!*

Furthermore, I should point out that the Bible repeatedly uses the terms "soul" and "spirit" interchangeably. In John 12:27, Jesus said, *"now is my soul* (Greek: ψυχή) *troubled."* In an almost identical context in the next chapter, John says that Jesus was *"troubled in spirit* (Greek: πνεύματι)" *(John 13:21).*

Another example of interchangeability like this would be Mary's words that are recorded in Luke 1:46-47: *"My soul (Greek: ψυχή) magnifies the Lord, and my spirit (Greek: πνεῦμά) rejoices in God my Savior."* The terms are synonymous in this context.

Note also that when speaking of death, the Bible uses "soul" and "spirit" interchangeably to refer to what departs to be with God. Of the rich fool: *"This night your soul (Greek: ψυχή) is required."* However, Stephen prayed, *"Lord Jesus, receive my spirit (Greek: πνεῦμά)."* It is very clear from a contemporary standpoint that the evidence that "soul" and "spirit" are interchangeable; any supposed distinction is purely artificial.

They believe that those who propose the trichotomist view, that man is composed of body, soul, and spirit, have simply been very careless in examining the Biblical data. They have focused on a couple of passages and ignored the vast body of Old Testament and New Testament material that clearly demonstrates that the terms are synonymous.

Many contemporary theologians would agree that the trichotomist view is also a problem since it is typically used to support the erroneous idea that God communicates mystically with our "spirits" and thus bypasses our intellect or mind. However, the "heart" cannot fully rejoice in what the intellect does not comprehend, and this false teaching quite often leads people to swallow false and destructive heresies as well. The trichotomist view is employed to authenticate all kinds of far-fetched "revelatory prophecies" from false teachers like those in the Word of Faith and Prosperity Gospel movements.

The teaching that man is two parts or a unified dichotomy of body and soul/spirit helps to avoid these errors, and more importantly, is faithful to Scripture.

So, does it make a difference which view about the nature of man we hold?

The answer may be to some that yes, it does make a difference because the view that man is merely a material being (naturalistic materialism) undermines the Biblical truth that we were made in God's image to know God. As for me in regards to eliminating toxins, the point is still crystal clear: we must rid ourselves of ALL toxins, and every part of our being is in need of cleansing every so often. There are many things we can do to purge ourselves of unwanted toxins. I have three specific things that will carry us a long way toward great health. The first is . . .

Be refilled with the power of the Holy Spirit.

And be not drunk with wine, wherein is excess; but be filled with the Spirit. (Eph. 5:18)

But ye, beloved, building up yourselves on your most holy faith, praying in the Holy Ghost. (Jude 1:20)

There's nothing better for an emotional and spiritual cleansing like being in the presence of the Most Holy and His Holy Spirit. All of our spiritual power comes from God's Holy Spirit. We need to be in His presence for to cleansing and to recharge.

List a few ways that you can come closer to God by being refilled by the Holy Spirit:

_____

_____

_____

_____

_____

Go on a *Negative News* fast.

Don't think that avoiding the network news is enough with this step. You'll need to disconnect yourself from people who perpetually bombard you with the negative news of what everyone else is doing. You know what I'm talking about. Make a list of ten negative people in your life who are currently toxic to you:

_____

_____

_____

_____

_____

_____

_____

_____

_____

_____

Taking a break from social media is often necessary as well. Whatever services are perpetuating that negative feeling inside of you have to go. Address the sources and distance yourself for a period of time. You might feel so good when doing this that you make it a permanent life change.

> *Finally, brethren, whatsoever things are true, whatsoever things are honest, whatsoever things are just, whatsoever things are pure, whatsoever things are lovely, whatsoever*

things are of good report; if there be any virtue, and if there be any praise, think on these things. (Phil. 4:8)

If the information that you're receiving doesn't align with these eight characteristic filters, then simply discard it.

Learn to quiet your mind.

Be still, and know that I am God: I will be exalted among the heathen, I will be exalted in the earth. (Ps. 46:10)

Quit putting so much junk into your mind and body. We tend to do, think, and feel too much. Learn to live more simply. You'll enjoy life more and have less to worry about. By limiting the amount of stuff entering your body and mind, you'll have fewer toxins bombarding you. And with all things, lean on God when questioning what must stay and what must go. List ten ways that negative toxics are coming into your life that must be eradicated:

_____

_____

_____

_____

_____

_____

_____

_____

_____

_____

THE NEW CLEAN YOU

There is no better time than now to create a better, new you. Even if you believe yourself to be content with who you currently are, there's always room for personal improvement. Your Father above does not expect you to be perfect. However, He does understand how the enemy operates. Allowing yourself to be content allows toxins to settle into your glass. Be sure to do all that you can to refill your glass with pure, clean water each day. You will gain a happier, better, more full life.

CHAPTER 2

What a Pity

Toxins are the unclean and oftentimes poisonous disturbances that wreak havoc on our bodies and lives. The Lord wants better for us, and we should want better for ourselves.

The word *want* is one of particular peculiarity. When we want something, it usually means that we will do most anything to get it. But what makes the situation of *want* so peculiar is that many times **we** are the driving force behind the reason for not getting what we want. Yes, too often we are our own worst enemies regarding attaining that which we want, desire, or need. This same position holds true in regard to allowing toxins to enter our lives. None of us want to allow toxins in, yet we are the ones constantly opening the door to them.

There are enormous amounts of toxins that can enter into our lives. Perhaps the worst kinds are spiritual and emotional toxins. In this chapter I will make you aware of a special toxin that way too many people of this world open their doors to. That toxin is the self-defeating emotional toxin called *self-pity*. Perhaps the vilest toxin we can allow into our lives is self-pity—seeing ourselves as victims. It's one thing to be victimized by someone or something. It's entirely another matter doing it to yourself. Self-pity is an unnecessary toxin.

It's not the will of God for us to live as victims. God tells us that we are to live as victors as we overcome this world.

WHAT A PITY

*. . . for everyone born of God overcomes the world. This is
the victory that has overcome the world, even our faith. (1
John 5:4 NIV)*

Can you remember the first time that you dove off the high
dive at your local swimming pool? You stood at the edge of the board
afraid to jump. You worried about what it would feel like to hit the
water from such a high jump. You may have even wondered if you
would regret not jumping if you didn't go through with it. If you did
jump, however, it was the best thing for you because you learned to
have victory over that moment realizing that God was with you.

That's exactly what needs to happen today. You are standing at
the edge of something that God has called you to do. You might be
analyzing it to death, running through every possible scenario of what
that jump means to your life, but there comes a time when you just
need to take the leap of faith. It might even be that it is the Holy Spirit
behind you urging you to go. He might even be the One who is giving
you that little subtle shove into your destiny. Understand that it is
done for your own benefit. You can neither accept a victim mentality
nor should you live with a woe-is-me-pity-party mentality/attitude;
rather, know that God will be with you to the end.

*David also said to Solomon his son, "Be strong and
courageous, and do the work. Do not be afraid or discouraged,
for the LORD God, my God, is with you. He will not fail you or
forsake you until all the work for the service of the temple of
the LORD is finished." (1 Chron. 28:20 NIV)*

Finally, one of two things happened. You either ended up in
the water or you didn't. Either you overcame that fear then and there,
or the odds are you still haven't learned to jump and are still crippled
by such a fear.

WHAT A PITY

Too many people walk through life playing the role of a victim, feeling as if the entire world is against them. They blame other people for all the bad happenings in their lives. Succumbing to this emotional evil leaves them feeling inadequate, like they are doing something wrong, or even worse that the Lord is not there to help. Feeling all alone in the storms of life creates an emotional weak spot, which in turn causes so many of us to reason it away, often illogically. Too often the result is pitying ourselves.

The poison that is self-pity is not a new toxin to mankind. A few thousand years ago there was a boat full of emotional stalwarts who found themselves in a desperate situation. Instead of having faith in their Savior who slept a few feet from where they stood worrying, they chose to feel sorry for themselves. They doubted their Savior who had already done so much for them. Caught in the middle of a horrible storm in the middle of the Sea of Galilee, the apostles wondered to themselves why Jesus had saved their lives so many times before, only to allow them to drown at sea. Worried and without faith, they ran to Him and woke Him up saying, *"Teacher, do you not care that we are perishing?" (Mark 4:38 ESV).*

Now think about this situation. Jesus was on that boat with them. If the sea were to take the ship over, then Jesus too would have perished in the sea. After witnessing many miracles performed by the Lord, why then in that moment was their faith so shaken? The answer is that all of us succumb to fear—fear that leads too often to pitying ourselves. We allow ourselves to become victims to all that this carnal world offers.

That victim mindset can become a habitual way of looking at life. Bearing this shortcoming makes a person consistently feel as though he or she is unfairly getting the short end of the stick. People develop the belief that they are always being taken advantage of. Possessing this mindset leaves a person feeling powerless in confronting circumstances. This toxic attitude lets people believe that

32

no matter what happens, it will never be their fault. It releases them from responsibility, which may be a liberating feeling but is also a toxic behavior.

Today the victim mentality has become much too prevalent in our society. It has robbed this generation of the joy of taking complete responsibility for their own lives and actually achieving something that's positive, helpful, and productive. The victim mentality has become one of the greatest thieves to the potential God has placed within people. It has stolen from them the opportunity to live the life they were created to live. People are not achieving the goals the Father has set before them because they are too interested in absorbing pity for the same things many others in this world may be facing.

The blaming mentality is not good for the soul. It leads people to feel as if they have no control over their lives. Before long they reach the verdict that they are not in charge of anything. When you're not in charge, it's easy to deflect responsibility. Success or failure has nothing to do with their own actions, they think. This illogical understanding means that all that happens to them, especially the negative things, are brought about by everything except themselves, so when it all goes bad, they have a woe is me, "pity me" mentality.

Back to our story of the men in the boat. They ran over to the Lord and frantically woke Him up saying, *"Save us, Lord; we are perishing"* (Matt. 8:25 ESV). Jesus awoke, and He was confused. What was their problem? Why were they worried? He said, *"Why are you afraid, O you of little faith?"* (Matt. 8:26 ESV). The men were acting like victims. Why? They had the only man who was capable of saving anyone at any time personally with them, yet they worried about their lives. They pitied themselves for their situation. They might have secretly blamed Jesus for putting them in such a dangerous situation. Too many of us today are acting just like the men in this boat with Jesus—having little or no faith and accepting no fault in their circumstances.

WHAT A PITY

There is too much God has prepared for you to waste your life blaming others. God does not want you to live like a victim. He created you to be victorious!

> But thanks be to God, which giveth us the victory through our Lord Jesus Christ. (1 Cor. 15:57)

> . . . **in all these things** we are more than conquerors through him that loved us. (Rom. 8:37; emphasis added)

> Now thanks [be] unto God, which **always** causeth us to triumph in Christ . . . (2 Cor. 2:14: emphasis added)

> I can do **all things** through Christ which strengthens me. (Phil. 4:13; emphasis added)

Jesus has the power over everything. Through our faith in Him we are undefeatable! He rose from His slumber and faced the ominous storm. Spreading out His arms He yelled, *"Peace! Be still." (Mark 4:39).* And then there was a great calm. The sea became as smooth as glass, and the clouds were there no more.

Through our Lord and Savior Jesus Christ we have all the power we will ever need. There's no need to be a victim or pity yourself for the current circumstances of life that you may find yourself in. You are strengthened by the Lord! The Bible has made it clear that we, as believers, are not to live this life with a victim mentality. There's no need for a person to pity themselves because of the power of Christ. Notice the point of each of the Scriptures we just reviewed. Romans 8:37 says it all—through Him we are conquerors. It is He who *"causeth us to triumph in Christ"* *(2 Cor. 2:14; emphasis added).* And we *"can do* **all things through Christ***" (Phil. 4:13; emphasis added).*

The Lord Jesus is our example. We are to try and imitate Him in all ways. He doesn't act like a victim. He didn't run from the

WHAT A PITY

horrifying death on the cross. He knew what was coming but still took full responsibility for something He didn't even do—sin. He epitomizes strength over a situation. He's in control and does not let a situation make a victim out of Him. He accepted His fate for us with no pity for Himself.

Victims blame other people for what happens to them, yet look at how Jesus responded in the face of finality.

> *And Jesus said, "Father, forgive them, for they know not what they do." (Luke 23:34 ESV)*

Be honest, how would you respond if put in Jesus' position at Calvary? Would you die the death needed to cleanse this world? Or would you worry and complain, giving every excuse possible to get out of being crucified? The odds are that you would do and say anything possible to escape that terrible sentence. It's because you—like most people—have this commonly shared victim mentality. People just don't sacrifice their lives for others.

Victims tend to think only of themselves and the crises of their lives. Yet while hanging on the cross in the most unbelievable pain that anyone had ever endured, Jesus wasn't thinking about Himself. He was thinking about others like **you**. He was thinking about the thief on the cross next to Him.

> *And he said unto Jesus, Lord, remember me when thou comest into thy kingdom. (Luke 23:42)*

> *And Jesus said unto him, Verily I say unto thee, Today shalt thou be with me in paradise. (Luke 23:43)*

He was thinking about His mother Mary.

WHAT A PITY

When Jesus therefore saw his mother, and the disciple standing by, whom he loved, he saith unto his mother, Woman, behold thy son! (John 19:26)

Then saith he to the disciple, Behold thy mother! And from that hour that disciple took her unto his own home. (John 19:27)

Jesus became the victim so you wouldn't have to. He was able to do it because He saw beyond the pain of the cross. He saw the prize of the world whose sin could be forgiven, a world that could be redeemed and could spend eternity in the presence of the Great I Am. He saw beyond the pain of the betrayal of His dear friend Judas . . . the pain of the denial of His closest disciple Peter . . . the pain of the terrible lashing from the Roman soldiers . . . the ultimate crucifixion at the hands of His own people. The greatest question to be asked is, how did He do it?

Looking unto Jesus the author and finisher of our faith; who for the joy that was set before him endured the cross, despising the shame, and is set down at the right hand of the throne of God. (Heb. 12:2)

He could endure it all because of the love He had for you. He was the ultimate victim sacrificed for your victory. Knowing this, how can we ever believe that we are in any way worthy to be called victims? Not with all that has happened before us and with all the power of the Lord we have in us. Through Christ we can do all things (Phil. 4:13)!

That is how it should be. Why then do so many people still fall into the trap of a victim mentality? Despite what Jesus has done for us and despite what God's Word promises, there are still so many people who defeat themselves with pity and limit their lives, choking because of the toxic effects of the victim mentality. People still blame others for their lack of success. They blame the environment, the economy, and everything else for how they feel and their problems in life.

It's a sad situation, one that must be combatted. To do this we must first know two things . . .

Why people carry a victim mentality, and **How we should deal with people who carry a victim mentality**.

<u>Why People Carry a Victim Mentality</u>

Let us begin with answering why people may feel they need to carry a victim mentality. The first thing we need to know is that everyone has been the victim of something at some point in time, but not everyone has chosen to live with a victim mentality. Everyone reading these words at some point has been treated unfairly. Each person has been unjustly accused of something he or she didn't do. The odds are that you have been rejected by someone whom you thought loved you and whom you believed would be there for you forever but left you.

At some point you have been disrespected or rejected. We could probably go on and on with the slights you have endured. But get this, you aren't the only one who has had to deal with such things. You aren't unique in having those misery moments. We all have been there. Any one of us could choose to live the rest of our lives in self-pity because of what happened to us. The great news is that most of us choose not to live as a victim wallowing in self-pity.

Regrettably, there are those who do constantly live in self-pity. The question I pose to you is this: why do they carry that victim mentality? I believe there is a three-part answer.

WHAT A PITY

Reason #1: Human Nature Enjoys Self-Pity

No matter who you are, there's a chance that a spirit of sorrow will be upon you. It's an emotional spirit that can take control of you, causing you to see yourself as a victim. Allow me to give you a prime example from the Bible of someone who allowed self-pity to take over his life. It got so bad that his emotional outburst caused him to murder someone.

> Ahab said to Naboth, "Let me have your vineyard to use for a vegetable garden, since it is close to my palace. In exchange I will give you a better vineyard or, if you prefer, I will pay you whatever it is worth." But Naboth replied, "The LORD forbid that I should give you the inheritance of my ancestors."
>
> So Ahab went home, sullen and angry because Naboth the Jezreelite had said, "I will not give you the inheritance of my ancestors." He lay on his bed sulking and refused to eat. (1 Kings 21:2-4 NIV)

The king was a powerful man who could've had anything. When Naboth refused him, the king was so overtaken by pity that he went to his room and moped. He wouldn't eat or drink. The ruler of a kingdom was acting like a spoiled child, feeling bad for himself because he wasn't getting what he wanted.

So full of himself was the king that he was made happy again only when his wife, the evil Jezebel, created a plan to have the landowner murdered.

Self-pity is an emotional toxin that will take over your sense of reasoning and rationality. This evil king was so overwhelmed by feeling slighted or wronged that he allowed another man to die. The emotion separated him from reality. It's what it does. Feeling sorry for yourself will either paralyze you or push you toward atypical behavior. Either way, you are not being the child of God you are supposed to be if you are controlled by self-pity.

Understand that you cannot always control what has happened to you in life. However, you can *always* choose whether what happens to you will control you. I like to say that life is 10 percent of what happens to you and 90 percent of how you react to it. That is exactly where too many people are living right now. They are letting what has happened to them control their minds and their emotions. This misdirects where they are going in life.

Self-pity becomes a medication we take to alleviate the pain of rejection or disappointment. The reality is that self-pity causes us to think more of ourselves than for others. Doing so may contradict what the Bible teaches us to do.

> *For I say, through the grace given unto me, to every man that is among you, not to think of himself more highly than he ought to think; but to think soberly, according as God hath dealt to every man the measure of faith. (Rom. 12:3)*

Reason #2: Human Nature Avoids Responsibility

What makes self-pity a toxin is that it strips us of our responsibilities. Life is much easier when we blame someone else for our mistakes and faults. Too many people push their blame onto the next person. There are a plethora of instances of this happening throughout the Bible.

Adam blamed Eve for his sin.

> *And the man said, The woman whom thou gavest to be with me, she gave me of the tree, and I did eat. (Gen. 3:12)*

Cain tried to dodge the responsibility of killing his own brother.

And the LORD said unto Cain, Where is Abel thy brother? And he said, I know not: Am I my brother's keeper? (Gen. 4:9)

Pilate attempted to absolve his guilt at the crucifixion of Christ.

When Pilate saw that he could prevail nothing, but that rather a tumult was made, he took water, and washed his hands before the multitude, saying, I am innocent of the blood of this just person: see ye to it. (Matt. 27:24)

People carrying a victim mentality do not want to own up to who they are and what they've done. Often they will look for a support, an excuse to push blame. They won't take personal responsibility for their actions but will blame it on someone else. They seem to always refuse to take responsibility for the consequences of their own actions.

The difference between a grown-up and a child is responsibility.

When I was a child, I talked like a child, I thought like a child, I reasoned like a child. When I became a man, I put the ways of childhood behind me. (1 Cor. 13:11 NIV)

Putting away childish things means holding ourselves accountable for all that we say, think and do. It's a difficult task but one that is essential as a servant of God. The Lord desires for us to be responsible. If we are not, if we allow this toxin to remain, it hinders His ability to fully use us.

Reason #3: Human Nature Seeks to Justify Detrimental Behavior

There's a cycle to toxicity. It's a revolving door where people justify the silly or selfish actions they carry out. An alcoholic will justify his drinking by blaming it on the hurt of an abusive father. The drug addict may justify her abuse of prescription drugs, blaming that she was not accepted by the other kids throughout school. Emotional seclusion and alienation in her youth allows her to justify harmful actions as an adult. It's a process called victimization.

Victimization—"the process of making a victim of," is dangerous for various reasons. It blinds you by denying reality. It causes you to fail to learn what's happening to you. It <u>justifies your suffering</u>, making an easy way out from challenging yourself and growing from within. Victimization <u>gives you that sense of entitlement</u>; you believe you have some sort of privilege that others do not have. <u>It's a discriminatory action</u> that not only upsets others, it also fools you into believing that things are worse for you than for others. It's a self-defeating belief. And finally, <u>victimization slowly takes you over</u>—it becomes who you are. You move from "feeling" like a victim to actually "being" one.

<u>How We Should Deal With People Who Carry a Victim Mentality</u>

When we want answers to any question, we need only to look toward the Lord's handbook—the Holy Bible. When wanting to know how we should deal with people who carry a victim mentality, we must look to our best source, the Lord. He is the wisest One of us all and has many stories that teach us many things. One such example comes to us regarding an old cripple with many excuses of why he was never healed.

Jesus came to the Pool of Bethesda and found a man of interest in John chapter 5.

One who was there had been an invalid for thirty-eight years. When Jesus saw him lying there and learned that he had been in this condition for a long time, he asked him, "Do you want to get well?" (John 5:5-6 NIV)

The man had been there by the healing pool for many years. We also know that because he had been sick for so long, his sickness had become part of who he was, his identity. The longer we allow ourselves to live with emotional pain, the greater the chance that the sickness (toxicity) will work its way into who we are.

If you think about it, I'm sure you'll realize that you too deal with people who don't remember the last time they didn't know suffering. Anger, pity, and lack of responsibility has been allowed to fester in them, causing them to endure emotional pain. They probably can't even remember what it feels like to really taste freedom from that kind of oppression.

The old man at the pool was certainly frustrated by his circumstances. He had no clue as to the blessing that would soon be coming his way. Jesus asked him, *"Do you want to get well?" John 5:6b*

Stop here for a moment. We know the man had an infirmity for many years. But a question was put to him, making him decide how he was going to live out the rest of his life. Jesus basically asked *Do you want to be healed or not?* This is what we need to do to help others rid themselves of toxicity: ask them if they really want to be healed. If so, here are some basic steps of how to do that.

Step 1: Do They Want to Be Delivered from a Victim Mentality?

If a person does not want to be delivered or feels as if he or she has nothing wrong within, then you are wasting your time attempting to help the person get set free. There has to be a personal desire and willingness for renewal to take place. A person must crave a new spirit. Look at how the victim mentality comes out of the old man. He responds to Jesus' question with this long, drawn out proclamation of excuses. All the Savior needed was a "Yes" or "No."

"Sir," the invalid replied, "I have no one to help me into the pool when the water is stirred. While I am trying to get in, someone else goes down ahead of me." (John 5:7 NIV)

Let's be honest: if he really wanted to be healed, he could have found a way to get into that pool before anyone else. He could've paid someone, promised them money as soon as he was able to work. He could have said, *Shove me in that water before all others, and I guarantee I'll make it worth your effort.* If it were truly his top priority to be healed, I believe that he would have found a way. I'm sure I would have. I would have begged, borrowed, or bribed someone to help me. Whatever it took to get into those healing waters is what I would have done.

That's not what this man did, though. He remained a victim of circumstances because that's where his heart was. He was comfortable being a victim. He obviously accepted it. This man was so limited in his thinking that the only thing he could answer Jesus with was the story of how impossible it was for him to be healed. This is where victim-minded people live. They focus on the problem and never on a solution. Subconsciously they don't want a solution because with it goes their pity from others. Pity is akin to love. The two share similar attributes. Each makes a person feel as if another person cares. Not to mention that with pity comes attention. These days everyone seems to crave attention whether it's misguided or not.

Jesus didn't ask the old man why he wasn't healed. He didn't even ask how he got sick. The only thing he asked was, *"Do you want to be healed?"* Jesus didn't ask for the man's story. He didn't introduce an avenue for the old man to blame others for his condition or bring forth any excuses. He just asked if the guy wanted to be healed. It's a yes or no answer. It almost seems cold by today's standards. Jesus was getting to the root of the man's troubles. Either he wanted help or not. Did he want to be healed or remain a victim? This same question is being asked of each one of us today. All of us have that little something that we have yet to rid ourselves of. We are all victims in some sense. And Jesus keeps asking if we want to be healed.

There are some people who don't want to be healed. They get more attention by playing the victim than they would if they were healed. Pity can be just enough of a comfort for some people to happily live in. It will suffice and keep them content. But it is nothing compared to love. Plus, getting away from a victim mentality takes work. Tearing down roadblocks that have been standing in the way for years takes God, which in turn takes prayer and faith. Some people are too comfortable with their demons. They'll settle for a life full of emotional melancholy. A person has to want change to rid themselves of the victim mentality.

Step 2: Don't Enable Them to Cling to Their Victimization

Jesus just asked and demanded that the old man stand, pick up his mat, and walk.

> Then Jesus said to him, "Get up! Pick up your mat and walk." At once the man was cured; he picked up his mat and walked. The day on which this took place was a Sabbath . . ." (John 5:8-9 NIV)

No longer was Jesus allowing the man to cling to his story, to his comfortable past. He demanded that the man get up and walk.

If we allow people to cling to excuses, to their story, they will keep telling it. Remember, the more a lie is told, the more the teller will believe it. Most of the time the story they tell is not the story God has for them.

Jesus healed the old man. He not only healed him but also made him completely whole in every area of his life: physically, spiritually, and emotionally. The reason I believe this is that later when Jesus sees him again,

Later Jesus found him at the temple and said to him, "See, you are well again. Stop sinning or something worse may happen to you." (John 5:14 NIV)

He was made whole. Why? Because Jesus knew he was in need of more than just a physical healing. He needed spiritual cleansing as well.

The Lord warned the man about going back to his old ways. *"Don't go back to the victim mentality,"* He was saying. That kind of mentality will lead to something worse than what befell you before.

The reason so many people are not healed is because we let them keep telling their story without ever correcting them. We excuse, justify, ignore, deny, or reason away needing to help them escape their victim mentality. We must be the ones who force the hands of those saturated by toxic ways. We must not allow them to avoid the help they need. We must bring them to a place where we don't solve their problems; we must bring them to the feet of Jesus to be healed fully.

Don't let them talk about how they have been victimized. Rather, help them create a new path, a new story: one of salvation, clarity, and love.

Step 3: Don't Let Them Become More Dependent on You Than God

Victim-minded people tend to depend on other people for validation. They will tell you a story over and over again about how they were wronged. They do this because they need you to validate them and make them feel special.

There is a time for encouraging words. Still there must also be a time when people realize that their validity shouldn't come from those around them. It comes from God.

45

Having predestinated us unto the adoption of children by Jesus Christ to himself, according to the good pleasure of his will..." (Eph. 1:5)

Behold, what manner of love the Father hath bestowed upon us, that we should be called the sons of God: therefore the world knoweth us not, because it knew him not. Beloved, now are we the sons of God, and it doth not yet appear what we shall be: but we know that, when he shall appear, we shall be like him; for we shall see him as he is. (1 John 3:1-2)

There's no doubt that there is a time to be there for victim-minded people. Still, there is also a time when those individuals (as believers) must learn to do for themselves. Having helped others rid themselves of toxic entities or ways, you now have entered into a relationship of co-dependency, where now they are depending on you to get them through difficult times. The problem is that they should be dependent on God, not just you. Victory rests in Christ alone. Of course, we must help when we can, but keep in mind that we are not taking God's place. We are helping others get to Him. Believe me, when they're really ready, He will do the work that must be done in that person.

CHAPTER 3

People Possessing a Manipulative and Domineering Spirit

Mary was a high school cheerleader who had aspirations of being a chef at a fancy restaurant. She loved to cook and would always dabble in her mother's kitchen, experimenting with various flavors. To her it was a great game that always ended with her and her loved ones enjoying her unique offerings. It was a win/win situation. Even if her culinary experiments didn't quite turn out the way she wanted, she still got to eat something different.

Mary, like so many high-schoolers, believed she was in love. Dave was the target of her affections. He was what many would call a "man's man." Joy to him started at 2 A.M. when he would ready himself for the hunt. Dave loved hunting just as much as Mary loved cooking.

Both Mary and Dave had plans to attend college. Those plans were shattered when their premarital sex resulted in a child. Instead of adventure and travel, Mary faced diapers and 3 A.M. feedings.

They were married and they had problems from the very beginning. Dave was a controlling man. Mary could go nowhere without him. Dave would still go to parties while Mary stayed at home with the child. A few years later the verbal and emotional abuse started. Mary's life did not turn out as she had hoped. Her husband controlled her and oppressed her at every turn.

PEOPLE POSSESSING A MANIPULATIVE AND DOMINEERING SPIRIT

I didn't tell you about Dave and Mary's life to give you a reason to dislike Dave or to root for Mary. I spoke of their lives to exemplify the spirit of manipulation and dominance. It's an evil spirit that poisons people of this world.

The sad truth is that far too many people act the way Dave does. Some people might be thinking that he is a terrible guy. The truth is, he is not. Dave possesses spirits that make him act the way he does. To be specific, he possesses manipulation and domineering spirits. Regrettably, there are a multitude of people around the world affected by these evil spirits.

Manipulative and domineering spirits are literally all around us. As faithful servants of the Lord, it is imperative that we learn to identify these entities rather than attacking the inhabited vessel that they may dwell in. It's also our responsibility to rid ourselves of these spirits and help others see, understand, and rid themselves of such toxic entities. Understand that manipulating and domineering spirits are unstable, poisonous, and geared toward separating people from God.

> Be strong and of a good courage, fear not, nor be afraid of them: for the LORD thy God, he it is that doth go with thee; he will not fail thee, nor forsake thee." (Deut. 31:6)

The reason you need to study this chapter so carefully is it teaches you about those possessing a manipulative and domineering spirit. These are the kinds of people who intimidate others as a means of getting what they want. Unfortunately, we will come across people with these spirits everywhere.

We might deal with them at work. It might be your boss who makes unreasonable demands and uses intimidation as a means of getting what he or she wants, or it might come from a coworker who

49

PEOPLE POSSESSING A MANIPULATIVE AND DOMINEERING SPIRIT

manipulates you, making you feel less than what you were created to be.

We might even have to face this spirit in church. I personally know a great minister who confessed to me that this particular spirit is thriving among many of his church members and church leaders. He explained that he had witnessed people pushing other members around and using them like chess pieces to get what they wanted and go where they wanted to go for their own personal benefit rather than for impacting the Kingdom of God.

There's a big difference between pushing someone to become better and pushing them so hard that they become bitter. There have been many people who have quit the church because they were manipulated and used by someone who was their spiritual authority. These people became casualties of demonic, intimidating, and manipulative spirits.

To combat this evil and oppressive spirit, it is my objective that by the end of this chapter you'll be better at recognizing and deflecting such things away from your life and from others' lives. You must be able to not only recognize these spirits but also effectively handle these spirits when they come your way. Being aware of the destructive things around us improves our ability to escape the traps they set for us. We also will be able to help others move away from or deal with these destructive powers.

The first thing we need to understand is that intimidation and manipulation are more than character issues. They are important and powerful *spiritual* issues. They often arise from the spiritual realm and spiritual beings, not just by our physical bodies.

There are two specific spirits that I've noticed that are attached to this type of toxic relationship. The spirits I'm referencing are the *Spirit of Leviathan* and the *Spirit of Jezebel*. Notice that there are no generalities here. We are speaking in specifics. These spirits are evil entities whose aim it is to hinder or snuff out the Christian way. They want to ruin salvation and eliminate the work that Christ did on the cross.

My hope is that by recognizing what these entities are and knowing what their purpose is, you will be able to overcome anything they do. This is part of the spiritual warfare that has been preached by every Christian minister and every believer knowing that they were at war with Satan. Do not be fooled into believing that we are in peaceful times. A war is constantly being waged between good and evil. You either fight for a side or become a spiritual prisoner of war.

The Spirit of Leviathan

So what is the Spirit of Leviathan? We learn that this was a sea creature that was alive and known to Job (see Job 3:8, 41:1-34). Job probably was alive around the time of Abraham (born around 2166 BC). We know that Job knew this creature from the way that God described leviathan to him. We can see in the first couple of verses the assumption that Job knew what the creature was simply by hearing its name. Job's response was not, "I have no idea what you are referring to, God!" Job 41 holds a good description for us.

> *Canst thou draw out leviathan with an hook? or his tongue with a cord which thou lettest down? Canst thou put an hook into his nose? or bore his jaw through with a thorn? (Job 41:1-2)*

In a literal sense, the leviathan is a twisting and coiling sea serpent that is nearly impossible to catch. Sounds like some sort of sea dragon, doesn't it?

> *In that day the LORD with his sore and great and strong sword shall punish leviathan the piercing serpent, even*

leviathan that crooked serpent; and he shall slay the dragon that is in the sea. (Isa. 27:1)

It sounds like the Bible is describing an earthly creature. But wait. There are also insinuations that this sea creature is spiritual in nature. There is a spiritual analogy that God reveals about him as well. Looking at the third verse of Job 41, we see an important reveal.

Will he make many supplications unto thee? will he speak soft words unto thee? (Job 41:3)

God is speaking, and He is asking Job if this enormous and powerful creature (read the rest of Job 41) entreats Job for mercy or speaks gently, or lets Job take it as a slave, or lets Job put a leash on it to make it a pet for little kids. These are hypothetical questions; the answer to all of them is no. The point is clear: no human can subdue this creature, but God can. Since that is so, God challenges, "Who then is able to stand against me?"

How then can a sea creature speak and petition us? The word *supplication* means a humble and earnest petition. According to God's Word, it seems as if this sea creature, this serpent, might be able to beguile people. Who else do we know as a beguiler?

And the LORD God said unto the woman, What is this that thou hast done? And the woman said, The serpent beguiled me, and I did eat. (Gen. 3:13)

We, of course, know that beguiler to be Satan. Is this Leviathan also of him?

The name Leviathan comes from the root word that means "to twist." That is one of this trickster's primary tactics. The spiritual analogy is one who will twist your words and make them mean something entirely different from what you intended. A person who is demonized, thus under the control of the Leviathan spirit, will twist the meaning of your words and seek to destroy the unity people have with one another. This spirit seeks to divide and conquer. It tries to divide and dismember the relationship God has connected you to within the body of Christ. Its aim is to foster an atmosphere of accusation against you. It wants to destroy your relationships.

Why is it that the Leviathan wants to destroy our relationships? It's because it is through our connections that we receive the love and strength we need to fulfill and reach our full God-given potential. Paul describes this bond like the joints of a body holding a person together.

> From him the whole body, joined and held together by every supporting ligament, grows and builds itself up in love, as each part does its work. (Eph. 4:16 NIV)

Unity within the circle of Christ is a bonding agent that holds together our love and protects against evil. The cohesiveness that the Body of Christ creates gives each of us the spiritual supply and strength we need to function properly and repel evil effectively.

The enemy will try to dislocate or divide these joints so our spiritual supply and strength will be weakened or outright cut off. One of the primary ways the devil does this is by twisting the words of someone to make you think something that's not true about them. The enemy is trying to separate us from our support.

When a pack of lionesses are on the hunt, they look for the weakest member of the pack. They then try to separate that animal from the rest of the herd. It's easier to kill that animal when all the others are not there to help defend it.

Satan's plan and his evil spirit that is the Leviathan are no different. He wants to twist the words of one person so the other person will take them completely out of context. Before the one

PEOPLE POSSESSING A MANIPULATIVE AND DOMINEERING SPIRIT

person knows it, the message is completely misconstrued to mean something both God and the speaker never intended for it to mean. The twisting of those words brings division between those two communicating and normally the entire congregation. The twist causes a ripple effect. People take sides. People start judging others. It can get ugly.

The Spirit of Leviathan doesn't only put one church member against another. Many times it is a husband versus his wife. This confrontational spirit is constantly attacking marriages. A wife wonders, *What did my husband mean by that?* Then with the right amount of spin, confusion, and suspicion, real harm ensues. The enemy twists things a little more each time. If we don't learn to discern what is happening here, we are soon left with a broken marriage, wondering what just happened.

I am fearful for the American people. I believe that the spirit of manipulation and dominance is weighing heavily on this people.

As the political discourse of this nation has been twisted to such a degree, it is nearly impossible for people to make a rational and reasonable decision because of the deception that has been brought to the forefront by this twisting and coiling spirit.

Even worse for the individual is that many of you reading these words right now are suffering from the attack of a Leviathan spirit. I bet you are being accused of things you are not guilty of. But I bet the words of the person making that claim against you sound reasonable or outright convincing to others. They might make you feel guilty even when you have no blame.

Actions and accusations like these cause you to lose your focus, to stress, and even to lose sleep. You become tormented by the twisted words, accusing looks, and unreal things whispered about you.

PEOPLE POSSESSING A MANIPULATIVE AND DOMINEERING SPIRIT

These accusations and worries lead you to wonder if you are in control or being controlled.

He that hath no rule over his own spirit is like a city that is broken down, and without walls. (Prov. 25:28)

The man who can't control his life from the inside will always have his life controlled by someone or something from the outside. You were not created to be controlled by circumstances or the devil. Neither are you created to be swayed by other people into being beguiled.

You have the Holy Spirit within you to give you the power to discipline your emotions and keep your mind and body under control. How many times do we hear the words, *"He makes me so mad!"* Really? That other person physically came over and required you to be mad? The devil made you lose control? You know that didn't happen. You became angry because you chose to. You listened to the lying words of that evil spirit and believed them because you chose to. Your choices made you act, feel, or respond in a particular way. You should've prayed to God, asking for clarity to see if you were being manipulated or fooled by an evil entity.

It's so important that we learn discipline and control over our emotions and responses. Otherwise, we become victims of the spirits around us. Giving the spirit of manipulation and oppression reign over us is a choice we make.

There's another choice: we can make the decision today that no one or nothing will ever control us again. We have the power through Christ to control ourselves. We have to learn to use it. We need only to recognize this spirit of Leviathan that's working against us. We also need to learn how to take full authority over it.

PEOPLE POSSESSING A MANIPULATIVE AND DOMINEERING SPIRIT

In that day the LORD with his sore and great and strong sword shall punish leviathan the piercing serpent, even leviathan that crooked serpent; and he shall slay the dragon that is in the sea. (Isa. 27:1)

Never allow the twisted words of the enemy to convince you that you are someone whom God never declared you to be. Satan is the master at twisting words and dividing relationships. It started for him in the Garden of Eden with Adam and Eve.

Now the serpent was more subtil than any beast of the field which the LORD God had made. And he said unto the woman, Yea, hath God said, Ye shall not eat of every tree of the garden? (Gen. 3:1)

. . . and it continues with us today. We cannot allow this conniving spirit to hinder our relationships with one another and especially with God.

Look at the six things God hates. But pay attention to the seventh thing, which is an abomination to Him.

There are six things the LORD hates, seven that are detestable to him: haughty eyes, a lying tongue, hands that shed innocent blood, a heart that devises wicked schemes, feet that are quick to rush into evil, a false witness who pours out lies and a person who stirs up conflict in the community. (Prov. 6:16-19 NIV)

There is very little chance of confusing the fact that God really hates those who sow discord among brothers. If you are trying to separate believers, well . . . you need to be delivered form the Leviathan spirit. It's that simple.

PEOPLE POSSESSING A MANIPULATIVE AND DOMINEERING SPIRIT

I'm pointing this fact out because you need to know that if God hates something, He'll create a way to combat it. As a matter of fact, I'm here today to tell you that you can be strong in whom God has created you to be in order to overcome this spirit. Jesus Christ is the only way to overcome this spirit. He is the way to overcome everything.

> *Nay, in all these things we are more than conquerors through him that loved us. For I am persuaded, that neither death, nor life, nor angels, nor principalities, nor powers, nor things present, nor things to come Nor height, nor depth, nor any other creature, shall be able to separate us from the love of God, which is in Christ Jesus our Lord. (Rom. 8:37-39)*

The Spirit of Jezebel

The other spirit that you need to be aware of is the spirit that attached itself to a woman named Jezebel. This spirit is not so subtle.

As I stated earlier, a cardinal rule of Biblical interpretation, as in the case of the interpretation of any written document, is always **"context rules."** My job as a Biblical expositor is always to determine the meaning that the original Biblical author—and ultimately God himself—intended a passage to mean.

> *Nevertheless, I have this against you: You tolerate that woman Jezebel, who calls herself a prophet. By her teaching she misleads my servants into sexual immorality and the eating of food sacrificed to idols. (Rev. 2:20 NIV)*

In the case of understanding what John was referring to when he wrote about Jezebel at Thyatira, I must carefully discern the specific details that John wrote so that my conclusion is in line with what he intended his readers to understand.

PEOPLE POSSESSING A MANIPULATIVE AND DOMINEERING SPIRIT

The most significant detail in the passage is in verse 20 where Jesus says (in my paraphrase), "But I have [this] against you, that you tolerate the woman (Greek: γυναῖκα) Jezebel." That Greek word always means either "woman" or sometimes "wife"—if the relationship being expressed is her relation to her husband.

John could have written either "spirit" (Greek: πνεῦμα) if he had intended this to be understood of a spiritual being, or more specifically "demon" (δαιμόνια) if he had intended this to be understood precisely as a demonic entity only. However, he did not; he specifically stated that she was a *human being, specifically a* woman who must have had a demon attached to her.

Whether her name was literally Jezebel, I really don't know for sure; I think that John is probably calling her by this epithet because of the associations with the Old Testament character who was known for her promotion of fornication and idolatry.

There are other clear clues that this is **not just a demonic power**. In verse 20 John clearly states that what this woman was doing was *teaching* (Greek: διδάσκει) Jesus' followers. We must further understand that demons do come into the church to "teach" God's children deception.

This is significant because the term used in the New Testament for demonic influence is Greek: δαιμονίζομαι, which is the Greek word from which we get our English word "demon." The Greek word δαιμονίζομαι means "to be under demonic influence." It occurs thirteen times, all in the Gospels. What can cause confusion here is that John is referencing the woman here, and not the demon.

Another interesting fact found in here is Jesus' statement in verse 21 that He has given her "time to repent." If this were only a demon, repentance would not be an issue at all! Demons are fully devoted to evil and beyond the possibility of repentance or redemption.

Another interesting fact worth noting is the judgment that Jesus is going to inflict on "her children": death (v. 23). If this woman "Jezebel" were actually just a demon, she 1) could not have children, since demons do not procreate, and 2) if she did have "child demons," they could not die.

In conclusion, <u>all of the textual evidence</u> in my opinion points to an unrepentant, female, human teacher, under the influence of a demon, thus, the title: Spirit of Jezebel.

The Spirit of Jezebel is also a manipulating and domineering spirit that has creeped its way into the church at large. It's more direct or bold than the beguiling entity we previously learned about.

> *Nevertheless, I have this against you: You tolerate that woman Jezebel, who calls herself a prophet. By her teaching she misleads my servants into sexual immorality and the eating of food sacrificed to idols.* (Rev. 2:20 NIV)

There was a literal person in this church where Jesus was bringing rebuke to the entire church because they allowed her a position of authority within the church. Whether her actual name was Jezebel is unclear. Please notice that Jesus was addressing the spirit who drove this woman rather than the woman herself. The reference is a prophetic parallel, the exact same kind of thing as when John the Baptist was implied to be Elijah in Luke 1:17. Just as the cousin of Christ was under the influence of a previous prophet, so too was this woman under an evil spirit.

There's a spiritual influence in society and the church that can rightly be called the Spirit of Jezebel. This spirit of oppression existed way before the queen Jezebel. She was so totally controlled by its

PEOPLE POSSESSING A MANIPULATIVE AND DOMINEERING SPIRIT

nature that she has become equated with this spirit of control, and for that reason Jesus uses the name "Jezebel" when addressing the spirit who was at work within this church of Thyatira.

Who exactly was Jezebel? Jezebel, at least the Biblical character, first appears in 1 Kings 16 when she married King Ahab of Israel. She was the daughter of Ethbaal, the king and high priest of the Baal-worshipping Sidonians. Those people were engrossed with obsessive sensuality and all manner of sexual deviancy.

Ahab was completely subdued and dominated by Jezebel. Jezebel introduced a special and evil kind of worship to the people of Israel, the worship of Ashtoreth. This goddess, represented in Canaanite culture by the moon, was a power-hungry goddess of love and sensuality. Through the influence of Jezebel, ten million Israelites left the worship of God for the worship of Baal and Ashtoreth. Only seven thousand people in the entire nation were strong enough to repel the pull of this seducing spirit. What an outstanding fact this is.

After learning of this, it should give you some insight into just how powerful a spirit this is. Knowing the power that is out there attacking us, we must learn the characteristics of such a spirit so that we can protect ourselves from it.

The Spirit of Jezebel has a personality like any other entity. Here are five attributes of that spirit that you should learn. Knowing these might allow you to recognize this toxic spirit.

It seeks control through manipulation.

It has a deep hatred of true spiritual authority.

It uses emotional pressure in its pursuit of power.

It uses subtle or gentle persuasion to gain influence and get close to those in control.

PEOPLE POSSESSING A MANIPULATIVE AND DOMINEERING SPIRIT

It then uses this position to gradually dominate.

The Hebrew word for Jezebel means "without cohabitation." The Spirit of Jezebel will not live or "cohabit" with those she cannot dominate and control. She will have no equal. Control is what this spirit hungers for. When we rebuke it or learn to stand against it, we defeat it, and it will move on to someone less willing to fight.

Jezebel is a spirit of control. She has her own characteristics, and we can teach ourselves to look for the signs that go hand-in-hand with her. Here are three steps of control that we must pay attention to so that we can overcome this toxic spirit.

So what are some **symptoms** of the spirit of confusion—Jezebel?

Symptom #1: Control Brings Confusion

Do you feel as if you can't make a clear and decisive decision because of the people around you? And because of that do you live in a constant state of confusion regarding who you are and what you should be doing? If so, then you might be under attack by the Spirit of Jezebel.

We need to be very clear as to what we are hearing from God. We must not live in doubt. We are not supposed to allow it into our hearts. We have to know who we are called to be.

Our spirit was created to house the Holy Spirit and Word of God. When someone else's words control us, it creates conflict with what our spirit was created for. As a result, we will have neither inner peace nor truly guided toward our God-given destination.

There's too much confusion within the church and her people today. This is because of this spirit and others like it. Too many believers just aren't doing what they should be doing. They are not

PEOPLE POSSESSING A MANIPULATIVE AND DOMINEERING SPIRIT

filling themselves with the Word of God, praying enough, or have yet to fully give themselves over to the Lord. All of these things and so much more leave little gaps in our souls that allow evil confusing spirits to penetrate. We must learn personal, spiritual control.

Symptom #2: Control Brings Frustration

The Spirit of Jezebel within our lives causes us to lose control and become frustrated in our faith. When we are under the control of someone else, that control is holistic. It does not only affect us physically but also emotionally and spiritually. Being affected in all avenues of our lives can be frustrating. For me it goes back to what Paul references in Romans 7:19. I'm paraphrasing, but he says, *"I know what I'm supposed to do, but I don't do it; even though I really want to do the right thing, I don't."*

The Spirit of Jezebel is a poison that frustrates whoever it can. Look at what it did to Elijah, the great prophet of God.

> *But he himself went a day's journey into the wilderness, and came and sat down under a juniper tree: and he requested for himself that he might die; and said, It is enough; now, O LORD, take away my life; for I am not better than my fathers. (1 Kings 19:4)*

Elijah was one of the greatest prophets ever. Yet after he received a message from Jezebel, this oppressive and powerful spirit, he was left so depressed and overwhelmed that he wanted to die! If Elijah could be fooled by this spirit, then how do we stand against it?

The answer is by being well-informed. When we allow someone to intimidate, frustrate, and discourage us, we may very well be taken over and our lives poisoned. But if we do not allow ourselves to be pulled away from who we know we are and focus on our faith in

God, that's when that spirit will neither have authority over us nor will it be able to attack us and prevail.

The Spirit of Jezebel is a deceiving spirit, relying on lies to fake us out so we wind up changing ourselves. Standing resolute and being on guard against evil spirits keeps us from being frustrated. We simply have to prepare for those attacks and remain convinced that the Lord will always have our backs. We must believe, however, that this spirit and others are created to control our lives and frustrate us.

Symptom #3: Control Brings a False Conformity

We are the masters of our minds. We have the choice who we will follow, what we will believe in, and what our lives will conform to. God is not a cosmic rapist. He doesn't force us to pursue Him. Satan knows this as well. It's why he sends his controlling spirits to confuse us and trick us into conforming to what he wants.

When we are controlled by a spirit of fear or intimidation, we find ourselves conforming to the opinions and desires of those doing the intimidating. We are not made to conform to any image other than God's. Like water, we will conform to that which we are closest to. Know this, if you're not being conformed to the image of God, then you are on your way to conforming to evil. There are no two ways about it. No one will be found straddling a neutral line at the end of days. You are either with God or against Him. You'll either be living a life for Him or one that is evil or fully conformed to the flesh.

For anyone not having found God, here's a revelation for you— you might very well be under the control of the evil one or one of his team mates. And if so, then you are in need of deliverance. If you've been living away from the Lord, there's a good chance you're inhabited by a domineering and possessive spirit. The good news is that help is available because the power of deliverance is within your grasp.

PEOPLE POSSESSING A MANIPULATIVE AND DOMINEERING SPIRIT

The First Key to Deliverance is The Renewing of Your Mind

The first key to deliverance from intimidation is this: the renewing of your mind. The word renewing in Romans 12 means to renovate. Think of your mind as a house that you've owned for many years. The wallpaper is ugly, and the stairs need to be fixed. To make it better, you need to upgrade. This means removing what is old and broken and replacing it with what is new and good. In spiritual terms, you need to forgo the flesh or your old way of thinking and focus on your spiritual affairs: renew your mind. In this case, the good is God.

We start off in our spiritual renovation by removing our old way of thinking. Only then can we put in a new one, which includes humility, love, and devotion. Out goes indulgence, hubris, and arrogance.

The renewing of our minds absolutely needs the power of the Holy Spirit. That power will help us get back to the kind of thinking that God created us for. We must get back to the state of mind He desires for us to have.

> For the Spirit God gave us does not make us timid, but gives us power, love and self-discipline. (2 Tim. 1:7 NIV)

The Second Key to Deliverance is To Possess the Spirit of Power

Next, we must possess the spirit of power. Here the word "power" is used the same way as it is in Acts 1.

> But you will receive power when the Holy Spirit comes on you; and you will be my witnesses in Jerusalem, and in all Judea and Samaria, and to the ends of the earth. (Acts 1:8 NIV)

Translation: The more we pray in the Holy Spirit, the more power and authority we will possess. The Book of Jude tells us to pray

64

in the Holy Spirit (Jude 1:20). Doing so embodies us with supernatural strength, enough to overcome an evil spirit.

The Third Key to Deliverance is To Possess the Spirit of Love

We must possess the spirit of love. The source of love is a strong enough power to drive out any spirit of fear, intimidation, or anything else. The reason for this is simple:

> There is no fear in love; but perfect love casteth out fear: because fear hath torment. He that feareth is not made perfect in love. (1 John 4:18)

If there's one thing I know, it's that nothing can take the love of God away from me, not even my own depravity. God's love is not flawed. It is not emotional, and it's not selfish. It's a perfect love because His love was demonstrated in the decision to give the best gift He had for our benefit, and we didn't deserve any of it.

> That Christ may dwell in your hearts by faith; that ye, being rooted and grounded in love, May be able to comprehend with all saints what is the breadth, and length, and depth, and height; And to know the love of Christ, which passeth knowledge, that ye might be filled with all the fulness of God. (Eph. 3:17-19)

The greatest thing we can know is the fullness of the love Jesus Christ has for us. God gave us the gift of His Son and His love. For when we receive Jesus Christ, we receive that spirit of love that should motivate and drive us toward Him in every way.

The Fourth Key to Deliverance is To Possess a Sound Mind

Finally, we possess a sound mind. We are thinkers. Sometimes that's a bad thing. Most of the time, however, it is what gives us the desire to chase God . . . the passion to hate evil . . . the need for something good. Satan and all of his toxins try to sway our minds by getting us to chase the flesh. Yet through sound reasoning and constant study of God's Word, we will build up ourselves to His good Spirit while avoiding evil ones.

So many people are under attack from evil spirits. They manipulate, frustrate, and intimidate us at every turn. They try to convince us that it's people we are at war with. We cannot accept this falsehood. The toxins in our lives are not fueled by people, but rather by evil spirits.

> For our struggle is not against flesh and blood, but against the rulers, against the authorities, against the powers of this dark world and against the spiritual forces of evil in the heavenly realms. (Eph. 6:12 NIV)

Remember this, when you feel like lashing out against people, you are not angry with them but at the evil manipulating them. You should instead strive to help that person, like by praying for them. Don't forget: toxic people are good people possessed by evil entities.

CHAPTER 4

Dealing with Emotionally Abusive People

Anytime we hear the word "abuse," our senses go on high alert. Maybe this is because most everyone knows someone who has been abused. Or maybe this is because we live in an era that no longer whispers about a bully but rather broadcasts it out onto every kind of media. Perhaps we have finally gotten it through our heads that any kind of abuse is toxic to all it touches. Whatever the reason, when learning to rid our lives of toxicity, we need to thoroughly consider finding ways to stop all manner of abuse.

There are many kinds of abuse that need to be addressed, yet there's one particular type I want to focus on: emotional abuse. Any kind of abuse is wrong. But the reason I want to discuss emotional abuse in particular is this kind of abuse may be difficult to recognize, both by the one doing it and those affected by it. With physical abuse we can see the bruising and scarring, but with emotional abuse the damage is on the inside, hidden from view. This makes it so much more difficult to deal with because many times people do not know damage is being done.

Making matters worse is that emotional damage does not heal the way physical bruises do. Unlike the physical bruises and scars that heal in time, emotional bruises and scars will many times last decades or even an entire lifetime without ever fully healing. People carry bruises and scars from some random conversation that they had many years ago that can remain for decades: something that is said to us in high, middle, or even elementary school can stay with us a lifetime.

DEALING WITH EMOTIONALLY ABUSIVE PEOPLE

The human spirit can endure in sickness, but a crushed spirit who can bear? (Prov. 18:14 NIV)

Emotional abuse occurs when something is said, implied, or done with the intention to inflict emotional pain on someone on a constant basis over an extended period of time. Let's be honest, in many relationships, there's a level of teasing we have with each other. But there's a line that many people, even believers, cross when this teasing becomes a pattern of insulting that individual, and it evolves into an emotionally abusive relationship.

Emotional abuse can take many forms: verbal insults, non-verbal rejection, neglect, and isolation. Emotionally abusive relationships make you feel as though you will never be good enough. Name calling, threats, and rumors spread about someone and poisons them from trusting people because they feel threatened, disliked, or intimidated. And it is a real issue even among so-called believers.

Although the Bible does not use the words "emotional abuse," there are many examples of it all throughout the good book.

The first example involves a married couple named Abigail and Nabal. Abigail was a beautiful and helpful woman, but her husband Nabal was known to be *"harsh and badly behaved" (1 Sam. 25:3 ESV)*. In layman's terms he was an emotionally abusive landowner. In the King James, Nabal is called "churlish," meaning cruel, severe, and obstinate. He was fierce and cruel to people, even those who were there to help protect him and his property.

But one of the young men told Abigail, Nabal's wife, saying, Behold, David sent messengers out of the wilderness to salute our master; and he railed on them. (1 Sam. 25:14)

Abigail lived under the emotional abuse of this cruel individual, yet she stayed faithful to him, even to the point of protecting him from being killed by David and his men after her husband insulted David and his group. It was because of Nabal's emotional abuse and hardened heart that God smote him, and he died. Abigail was blessed to become David's wife.

Another example of emotional abuse arises from the same time period as our last example. Jonathan was the son of King Saul and best friend of David. Yet this kind and understanding man endured constant emotional abuse from his father.

> Then Saul's anger was kindled against Jonathan, and he said unto him, Thou son of the perverse rebellious woman, do not I know that thou hast chosen the son of Jesse to thine own confusion, and unto the confusion of thy mother's nakedness? (1 Sam. 20:30)

King Saul was emotionally abusing his son because the king knew that David would one day take his throne. He was amazed that his son could be friends with the person who would be king when he (Jonathan) was in line for the throne. The king thought his son was ignorant and had no heart. King Saul was quick to berate his child and beat him down with insults and insinuations.

Unfortunately, seeing parents publicly humiliate their children is nothing new. In this age of technology it seems to be in vogue to capture all manner of humiliation and put it on the Internet. The instances of emotional abuse are growing and gaining popularity as if they were a form of entertainment. This evil activity is escalating in popularity.

My heart goes out to children when I see them in public places being verbally assaulted by a parent. Too many emotional floggings are being conducted within the public's view. It's not only embarrassing but also the effects are too often left stinging for decades. So many parents don't understand the long-term effect their words and actions have on their children.

DEALING WITH EMOTIONALLY ABUSIVE PEOPLE

The final example regarding Biblical characters involves Samson and Delilah. Delilah, through her consistent nagging of Samson, brought him to the point of emotional suicide.

> *And it came to pass, when she pressed him daily with her words, and urged him, so that his soul was vexed unto death... (Judg. 16:16)*

Delilah knew what she was doing. She was pushing Samson past the emotional edge so that he would sacrifice his integrity. He may have even known that she wanted to know all of his secrets so that she could hold sway over him in every way. Either way, her abuses were not physical. They were emotional.

The point of bringing up these Biblical examples is to show you that what may be happening to you today has affected God's people for thousands of years; you are not alone in your struggles.

What you must understand is that despite any problem you might have, there's a solution for it. God always has your back. You need only to trust Him and put your faith in Him. Part of your solution lies in this chapter. In order to combat emotional abuse, you need to know three things:

How to recognize emotional abuse.

How to handle emotional abuse.

How to avoid emotional abuse.

Learning these three skillsets, absorbing this information, puts you into a situation to avoid or correct emotional abuse. You might not believe this information is relevant to you, but maybe God needs you to help others.

Skillset #1: How to Recognize Emotional Abuse

The best way to recognize emotional abuse is to see its antithesis through the Word of God—Biblical love. Perhaps the most famous passage about love comes to us in the first book of Corinthians. I believe that in chapter 13 Paul makes clear the point that any level of emotional abuse is wrong and not pleasing to God. Look at what the Bible says love is.

> *Love is patient, love is kind. It does not envy, it does not boast, it is not proud. It does not dishonor others, it is not self-seeking, it is not easily angered, it keeps no record of wrongs. Love does not delight in evil but rejoices with the truth. It always protects, always trusts, always hopes, always perseveres. Love never fails.(1 Cor. 13:4-8a NIV)*

Love is patient and is kind; love does not envy. Emotionally abusive people are not patient people. They are quick to flare up with anger at the smallest offense. This abuse is the parent who yells at the child for spilling the milk at breakfast. It's the wife who yells at the husband for buying the wrong kind of bread at the store on his way home from work. It's the person who doesn't know how to speak a kind word or give a compliment to another person. Rather, they consistently berate those even in their own household.

Love does not boast; it is not proud. An emotionally abusive person is a very proud person, boasting of accomplishments and making you feel as though you are insignificant and inferior to them. They try to make sure you know how much better they are than you and how superior they are over you at everything. They are quick to point out your flaws and shortcomings—especially those of a physical nature. They like to make fun of your appearance in order to make themselves seem so much better.

Emotionally abusive people act so superior because they have this deep-seated inferiority complex. It's most often found that those who brag about how great they are are actually extremely disappointed in themselves. Realistically, they do not see themselves as winners. And the ironic thing is that usually something happened in their youth that caused them to take on this false bravado to cover up their insecurities. Typically a parent, coach, or other influential person harshly criticized them, completely changing their perspective of themselves. In other words, most people are emotionally abusive because they were emotionally abused themselves. It's a tragic cycle. Emotionally abusive behavior is an attempt to protect the pride and ego of the emotionally abusive individual.

It sounds crazy, but emotionally abusive people are very insecure people. They protect that insecurity with a proud and haughty spirit. The only way to make themselves feel good is by making someone else look or feel bad.

It always protects, always trusts, always hopes, always perseveres. (1 Cor. 13:7 NIV)

Emotionally abusive people do the opposite of what this Scripture is saying. They make you feel as if you are a liar because they question everything you say. They do it so much so that you may even start doubting yourself. They never see anything positive in any situation or any person. Instead, they speak negatively and pessimistically about everyone they come across. They are the proverbial rainstorm that can walk in a room and suck all the positivity right out of it. Do you know this kind of person, the person who walks into a room and dampens everyone else's spirit? Most people at least know one. I am hopeful that's not you, but if it is, then quit it!

It's important to note that you are not judging the *person,* but you are judging the *behavior.* Did you know that Jesus actually commanded us to judge? Jesus told the crowd in John 7:24, *"Stop judging by mere appearances, but instead judge correctly" (NIV).* He was challenging them to make a right judgment *about Him!*

DEALING WITH EMOTIONALLY ABUSIVE PEOPLE

In 1 Corinthians 5, Paul rebukes the Corinthian church for its failure to exercise judgment of a sexually immoral man in their midst. Paul plainly tells them, "I have already passed judgment on the one who did this." If such judgment is wrong, then Paul sinned. However, he did not; he was doing what they had failed to do.

In verse 12 he challenges them, *"Are you not to judge those inside [the church]? God will judge those outside."* In light of the rebuke for their lack of judgment of the sexually immoral man in their midst, his first question clearly expects a "yes" answer, and the second question expects a "no" answer. The sinner, who is outside the church, will always exhibit sinful behavior and rebellion against God; that is a given. Believers are called to live a holy life; when they fail to do that and bring dishonor on Christ and the church, believers are commanded by Christ to make a judgment. Jesus gives the steps for how this judgment is to be carried out by the church in *(Matt. 18:15-20)*.

> *We are hard pressed on every side, but not crushed; perplexed, but not in despair; persecuted, but not abandoned; struck down, but not destroyed. (2 Cor. 4:8-9 NIV)*

<u>You are never defeated until you accept defeat as a reality</u>. Think on that statement for a moment. Defeat doesn't have to be your reality. Yes, there are times when you may feel cast down. There are times you may feel distressed. But being cast down and distressed doesn't mean you are defeated. Defeat comes only when you accept defeat as your reality because at that moment you have chosen to stay cast down and distressed. You have been given a promise through Paul's experience in this verse that even though life may put you in a position of being cast down, you are not destroyed! Meditate on and memorize this verse. Quote it often to yourself and others, even to those who pummel you with abuses. Understand that they cannot defeat you unless you choose to be defeated.

I'm convinced more now than at any other time in my life that people need hope. They need it more than anything else. They have to know that there is a brighter tomorrow, that the abuses suffered today will not overshadow their greatness tomorrow, and that love is so very necessary for this strategy.

Love endureth all things. Emotionally abusive people don't last. They give up when times get tough. They'll leave you all alone. The reason for this is they are looking out only for themselves. Emotionally abusive people are selfish people.

This is a sad commentary but an even sadder reality if you are beginning to think that this emotional turmoil might be something you do. If you find any of these characteristics in your life, then you need to get on your knees and pray. Pray to God and ask Him to forgive you. Then run to the person you may have abused and seek their forgiveness.

The bottom line is that abuse is an attempt to control another person. Physical abuse is an attempt to control another person through hitting, kicking, grabbing, or pushing, whereas emotional abuse is an attempt to control another person using feelings as a weapon. It's all done in an attempt to control what is done or not done for fear of how the other person is going to respond.

Would you know if you were being emotionally abused or abusing others? Are you altering the decisions you make about important things in life because you are afraid of how another person will emotionally react to you? Are there things you know that you should be doing but are not because you know it will trigger an emotional response from someone you love? Are you being held emotionally captive and not allowed to move forward in life? If so, you need to understand that you have a choice in the matter. That choice is made possible by your Lord and Savior Jesus Christ. Look to the Word of the Lord for proof:

If the Son therefore shall make you free, ye shall be free indeed. (John 8:36)

You have been set free by the blood and sacrifice of Jesus. He didn't only come to set you free from sin, He came to liberate you from all imprisonment, including the emotional bondage you have endured.

There's no reason for you to live your life bound in an emotional prison held captive by an emotionally abusive person. You must not let the devil tie you up, keeping you bound in those figurative chains.

You are an individual with a plan and purpose already mapped out by your Heavenly Father. Now is the time for you to step into that plan and refuse to be held back any longer by emotional abuse and bondage.

Remember your source of victory.

The horse is made ready for the day of battle, but the victory belongs to the LORD. (Prov. 21:31 ESV)

I'm a huge proponent of preparation. In fact, I believe that God anoints what I have thoroughly planned, prepared, and protected. When I take the pulpit to preach or teach, I want to make sure I have invested the needed time to prepare a timely message for people. I believe the same is true in every aspect of my life; God wants us to work hard preparing ourselves for what He will bring into our lives. But there are plenty of times when unforeseen factors arise. It's in those moments when we should be happy to remember that true victory comes not from our preparation but by the hand of God.

Solomon tells us that even though the horses are prepared for battle, our deliverance is given by God. So work hard and be prepared for what may come your way in life. But when things move out of our control, we should be thankful that we have stayed in constant prayer with God and that He has us covered. It's by His power and not our preparation that we will overcome everything that opposes us.

Skillset #2: How to Handle Emotional Abuse

So what do we do if we find ourselves in an emotionally abusive situation? The first thing is to acknowledge it. Never feel that as a Christian we should ignore a situation or tolerate it. Being a loving individual does not mean that we must be an emotional punching bag. There are loving and Biblical options other than tolerating the status quo. Jesus doesn't expect one of His children to constantly turn the other cheek. The Bible also declared, *"An eye for an eye" (Ex. 21:24).*

I know that some may say that this is comparing apples and bulldozers. If you read the entire chapter of Exodus 21, Moses specifies that the eye-for-eye principle applies in cases of "serious injury." He is referring to murder or other serious bodily harm to a person.

In the Sermon on the Mount, Jesus contrasted the proper response of a follower of his to the way that the Pharisees interpreted the eye-for-eye injunction. If you look at Jesus' three examples: 1) a slap on the cheek—which is a personal affront, 2) the person who wants to take your tunic, and 3) someone who coerces you to walk a mile, you will quickly see that none of these examples qualify as murder or other serious bodily harm to a person, but they are minor personal offenses. They might upset you, but they do not kill you or maim you.

The Pharisees were wrongly applying an appeal for justice in a case of serious harm or death to petty personal offenses. Jesus is correcting their misapplication of the Law. In the case of minor personal offenses, Jesus definitely **does** "expect one of His children to constantly turn the other cheek." But when it comes to emotional abuse that may lead to something much bigger, then no, it's not to be tolerated. Let me explain.

DEALING WITH EMOTIONALLY ABUSIVE PEOPLE

Abuse is a learned behavior. If we allow this learned behavior to continue, it will continue on to the ones we love and the ones they love—on and on. It's our responsibility that when we see harm being carried out, we do something about it. Do you remember when the Lord tipped over the money changers' tables in John 2:13-16? He took action. Although our scenario is not exactly the same, we should never accept verbal or emotional abuses.

There are two reasons:

It dishonors God,

and

It will often lead to physical abuse.

Here's a fact: An emotionally abusive person is not walking in right fellowship with God.

Can two walk together, except they be agreed? (Amos 3:3)

An emotionally abusive person has lost connection with what the Bible commands regarding what it says about interpersonal relationships.

Submitting yourselves one to another in the fear of God. (Eph. 5:21)

A healthy relationship requires the involvement of two people each having his or her own fellowship with God and submitting to Him. If either person refuses to submit to God, that relationship will be evidenced by a refusal to submit to each other. Without that fellowship with God or the commitment to honor each other, there will be a definite breakdown in that relationship.

Any relationship plagued by emotional abuse will eventually have to choose one of three paths:

The abuser acknowledges his or her behavior and repents to God and the one who's abused.

The abused person walks away from the relationship—maybe permanently.

The abuse is tolerated indefinitely, and both people are hurt.

Because you cannot control the behavior of anyone else, I want to give you some Biblical steps to look at the behavior and responses that are under your control.

Be firm in what God says about you regardless of what "they" say about you.

Because much of emotional abuse is verbal and their control of you comes from what they say about you, it's important to remember that what someone says about you doesn't define you. It's what God says about you that really matters and is really true.

You are worthy through Christ.

The fight has already been won. You don't have to struggle to prove yourself to God because through Christ you have already been approved and accepted. People in emotionally abusive relationships feel as if they have to prove their worth to the other person because they are always being put down.

Can you imagine the lost work Paul would have had if he cared about what his fellow Pharisees were saying about him after he became a Christian? They definitely were abusing him emotionally. They certainly wanted to and did abuse him in other ways as well. Still Paul stood firm in Christ's message and felt worthy because of Christ's calling on his life. He knew he didn't have to prove his worth to God because all the work necessary was already performed through Christ's work at Calvary.

You are liberated through Christ.

To the praise of the glory of his grace, wherein he hath made us accepted in the beloved. In whom we have redemption through his blood, the forgiveness of sins, according to the riches of his grace . . . (Eph. 1:6-7)

This is very important, so please allow me to reiterate: Jesus didn't come to set us free in *some* ways; He came to set us free in *all* ways. This includes freedom from emotional abuse. The book of John puts it this way:

If the Son therefore shall make you free, ye shall be free indeed. (John 8:36)

There's no ambiguity in this text. Christ did it already. He set us free. Why then would we let someone who is so much His lesser put us in bondage, especially when we are His favored children?

You are favored through Christ.

But now thus saith the LORD that created thee, O Jacob, and he that formed thee, O Israel, Fear not: for I have redeemed thee, I have called thee by thy name; thou art mine. When thou passest through the waters, I will be with thee; and through the rivers, they shall not overflow thee: when thou walkest through the fire, thou shalt not be burned; neither shall the flame kindle upon thee. (Isa. 43:1-2)

Notice the Bible doesn't say you'll escape these things. Rather that you will walk through them, but they won't hurt you. There's nothing in this world that can damage what really matters to us, our souls, because we are under the divine protection of God.

When you confess to the world that you are protected by God, you will be amazed at how much less abuse accosts you. Declaring your patronage to the Lord aloud is like a shield of protection. The more people know you are favored by God, the more protection it seems that you'll have. Your level of confidence that comes from God will eventually cause the emotionally abusive person to give up in their quest for you. When they find out that they can't control you, they will either give up, submit, or move on.

Skillset #3: How to Avoid Being Emotionally Abusive

If you have seen any of the negative things written thus far evidenced in your own life, you need to honestly evaluate if you have become an emotionally abusive person. If you believe that you emotionally abuse others, you need to start your recovery by doing three things:

Take responsibility.

Repent for your behavior.

Respect others.

Step 1: Take responsibility for your abusive actions

Stop blaming others for your outbursts of anger. Stop blaming your job, friends, or environment for how critical you have become. What happens to you does not determine who you are. It's time to step up and take responsibility for your behavior. Examine yourself to see who you are and what you must do.

In Ephesians 4:22-32, the Bible gives specific instructions on how Christians should be living. He pointedly states in Ephesians 4 that the Christian should not engage in abusive actions:

1) No unwholesome talk

2) Only what is helpful for building others up according to their needs

3) Get rid of all bitterness

4) Get rid of all rage — sudden, explosive anger

5) Get rid of all anger — settled wrath or anger bent on revenge

6) Get rid of all brawling

7) Get rid of all slander

8) Get rid of all malice

9) Be kind

10) Be compassionate

These are powerful admonitions to take responsibility for our actions toward other people.

Furthermore, when referring to the Lord's Supper, the Bible says to

> . . . let a man examine himself, and so let him eat of that bread, and drink of that cup. (1 Cor. 11:28)

The Lord will not hold someone else accountable for your actions and attitudes. They are your responsibility, yours and yours alone. God expects us to give a true account of ourselves.

> So then every one of us shall give account of himself to God. (Rom. 14:12)

We need to be honest with ourselves and make the right changes because we will be judged on them all one day.

> *But I say unto you, That every idle word that men shall speak, they shall give account thereof in the day of judgment. (Matt. 12:36)*

Trust me when I say the excuse "It wasn't my fault" won't work today. It definitely won't work on Judgment Day.

Step 2: Repent of your behavior

Once you take responsibility for your abusive behavior, your next step is to seek forgiveness from those you have offended or abused. Ask them to forgive you. Yes, it will be hard because you'll have to set your pride aside, walk in humility, and admit that you were wrong, but it is totally necessary.

If you feel that the Lord is prompting you now to seek forgiveness from some, list their names here:

_____

_____

_____

_____

_____

Now go to that person or people and admit what you've done, asking them to forgive you.

After that ask God to forgive you. Pray to Him and seek forgiveness for the way you treated one or many of His children. Once you have done that, you must then forgive yourself. Now I know that this can be considered secular psychobabble, not Biblical truth because what I've noticed over the past couple of years that what I call "psychobabble" has infiltrated the American church to an incredible degree.

Secular, atheistic psychology has substituted seeking the forgiveness of God (whom we have offended by our sinful actions, by our transgressions of his moral law) with the concept of self-forgiveness. Because it seems to speak of spirituality, many Christians assume that self-forgiveness sounds like a good thing for a Christian to do. Of course, the Bible never mentions the need for self-forgiveness but constantly reminds us that we need the forgiveness of our heavenly Father first and foremost. Why? Because it is His moral standards that we have broken and, therefore, we need His forgiveness, *not just our own*!

However, guilt does sometimes continue to plague Christians even after they have sought God's forgiveness; the answer is definitely not only self-forgiveness but also an acceptance of the forgiveness that God has provided for us. If a person is constantly continuing to wallow in guilt and self-deprecation and condemnation, it is a matter of underbelief in God's promise, not a symptom of lack of self-forgiveness.

Of course this life is a journey, and we are going to make mistakes. What turns a stumbling block into a stepping stone is your willingness to learn from your mistakes, moving on, and not making the same ones again.

Understand that after your change of heart, you'll become a new person. God loves that. You cannot go back to being that old person, however. Repentance is a change of heart: you cannot go back to behaving the same way you did before your revelation. Anytime you might feel an ugly attack of abuse coming on, you need only to pray to the Holy Spirit. He gives us control and discipline over our lives.

Step 3: Respect Others

Because emotional abuse is an attempt to control others and make yourself look better than you are, you must learn to focus on others instead of yourself. Caring about the next person more than yourself is an example that Jesus showed us. He demonstrated the love we are meant to have for others. Even if you cannot burn with love for them right now, you must still learn to respect them.

> ... *not looking to your own interests but each of you to the interests of the others. In your relationships with one another, have the same mindset as Christ Jesus: Who, being in very nature God, did not consider equality with God something to be used to his own advantage; rather, he made himself nothing by taking the very nature of a servant, being made in human likeness. (Phil. 2:4-7 NIV)*

CHAPTER 5

The Toxic Spirit of Offense

There will come a time when you will be offended. You can believe that you will be offended by the words that someone says to you or someone close to you. It's not only words that will offend, I'm afraid. There are people out there in this world who will unwittingly offend you with every part of their being. Their mannerisms, tone, body language, all the way down to their foul breath, they are going to offend you.

It's a sad reality that it may always be this way. I say this because our Lord told us ahead of time that we would face these attacks. Trust in the fact that evil spirits wills use whatever means possible to get a foothold into your life to create havoc. One of those ways is to be tested/tempted by the spirit of offense.

> Then he said unto the disciples, "Temptations to sin are sure to come, but woe to the one through whom they come!" (Luke 17:1 ESV)

The offenses are on the way, my friends, He said. *Don't be surprised when you come against controversy because you are one of mine.* It's a warning, a foreshadowing from the Lord. We should be thankful to suffer for Christ *(Acts 5:41).*

Did you catch that I referenced a spirit here and was not simply talking about inconsiderate or disrespectful people? There is an evil spirit, a toxic spirit that comes to cause us harm. It's not a spirit from God. Rather it's one of evil—the devil. It's one that roams free attacking anyone *(1 Peter 5:8)*. It has a special yearning to attack those who follow the Lord.

Just for clarification: a believer may come under demonic attack or influence, to be sure, but Christians after Pentecost have the indwelling Holy Spirit working in them to enable them to triumph over demonic influence. A Christian who has strayed from the Lord most certainly may come under demonic attack more easily than a Christian who is truly grounded in Biblical truth.

Everyone who is a follower of Jesus Christ will come against some kind of opposition from the enemy. Every single person reading this right now has experienced it. The only question is, *have you recognized this spirit of offense*? Some of you are experiencing it right now in your lives: something that has been done or said that if not dealt with properly will plant a seed of offense in your spirit. If allowed to sprout, that seed will begin to grow and overtake your spirit and destroy you from the inside out. It's why I've called this chapter "The Toxic Spirit of Offense." People must never allow themselves to be controlled by the toxic people of this world or the spirits that inhabit them.

The good news is that we are not made to be destroyed by such a spirit. It's not the wrongful things that are said or done to us that will destroy us; it's how we respond to them. What I mean is we have to know how the enemy attacks us then know how to combat his attacks. In fact, I want you to write this down somewhere where you'll see it often and remember it.

Your promotion in life is directly linked to your tolerance of pain.

If you want to be promoted in life, you must be able to deal with the tough stuff that comes your way. People are going to hurt you. It's a fact. They are going to criticize you. They are going to ostracize you. If you can't handle the pain of being talked about, you'll never be promoted in the service you provide or the power you wield.

The people who are promoted to the corner office with the big paychecks are the people who are able to handle the tough situations and solve the problems that are set before them. You can't have the corner office with the great view of the city without being willing to take on the tough stuff that comes your way. That toxic spirit of offense will bombard you all day long when it knows you can't handle it.

If you are not willing to experience the pain, you should never expect the promotion. I believe the higher you go in life, the more you will become a target for things to be said about you and done to you that could easily cause offense to rise within you. Then what happens is the enemy often uses that offense as a doorway into your life; once there, it creates a stronghold which leads to a handicap.

God has begun to promote some of you, and you are moving up the ladder of influence in life right now. But with that promotion has come an onslaught of attacks from people you never expected they would come from. There has been a barrage of things done to you by those whom you thought supported you. The reason this happens is the enemy loves to get a foothold in your life using the spirit of offense. It's used to make you think ill of the person being used by the toxic entity. Your enemy wants you to become so offended that you quit doing that specific good work that God created you for altogether.

A problem too many of us run into when dealing with the spirit of offense is that we see the attack of the person attacking us as a personal onslaught. If a coworker is used by the enemy against you to offend you, the first thing that you do—because you don't know the spirit of offense—is shut down or limit your communication or relationship with that person. Why? Because you take their attack personally.

THE TOXIC SPIRIT OF OFFENSE

You believe that that coworker has it out for you. That person wants to ruin you and all of the great things you have going. He or she is jealous of your hard work and dislikes you. These and notions like these are how we see the people who confront us. We see things as if it were done because of personal reasons; although at times this may be true, we also have to realize that this attack may be driven by another entity altogether. We have to get away from this falsehood that every attack is a personal one. You need to understand that sometimes good people simply do bad things because of the spirit influencing them.

I want you to start living your life with this philosophy: It's not personal; it's purposeful!

What this means is that not all people are out to get us. Some just may have evil spirits driving them, causing them to accost us. But they are not all out to attack us just because they wish they had our job or spouse or house or car, etc. People are made in God's image. The more we love one another, the better off it may be.

If you see someone attacking you, understand who it really is. It's often not the person but rather a spirit of infirmity; a spirit like the one of offense. When you can see through that evil intent to the person being held captive, you will see the truth and still love the demonically driven person.

For the weapons of our warfare are not of the flesh but
have divine power to destroy strongholds. (2 Cor. 10:4 ESV)

But what if you realize that it's you who are the one under the influence of such a spirit? What should you do? If you are indeed being attacked, then it probably means that the enemy has realized that you have a performing role in God's good Kingdom. If you are worried only about you, then that enemy would have no desire to affect what you are doing because you are already operating on his team. If you are under the attack of the devil, then keep doing what you're doing. It must be affecting him.

I feel the devil's attack on me right now because of the good work being done through this book. Am I offended? Absolutely not. I expect to be under attack by evil spirits when pushing toward the advancement of God's Kingdom.

I'll tell you who is offended. Most of this new generation. I've never seen a generation more offended than the one we live in right now. People are offended over politics, religion, freedom, protest, and so much more. In fact, the list is almost limitless.

We need to understand that this comes down to more than just a few preferences we have that differ from others. It's not just the opinions of others that we battle. It's the conniving forces of evil that aim to trick us into believing that we should feel slighted or angry, that somehow our beliefs or opinions are so much better than all others. That spirit of offense is whispering in our ears saying, *"Are you really gonna take that?"* Understand that we are not arguing with people. We are in a spiritual battle.

> *For we wrestle not against flesh and blood, but against principalities, against powers, against the rulers of the darkness of this world, against spiritual wickedness in high places. (Eph. 6:12)*

I believe that the spirit of offense is a strategy created by the devil to restrict us from reaching our full God-given destiny. Offense is not just an attitude or feeling. It is a spirit from the enemy. There is just one Holy Spirit of God, but there are several spirits of the devil, which are called demons. The devil contaminates our souls with his evil entities so as to hinder and keep us down. The devil knows if he can get you offended over someone or something, you will waste all of your creative energy trying to get even with or seek justice over the person who has offended you rather than fulfilling your calling.

How many people have you seen waste so much of their efforts trying to get even with someone because they feel they have been offended? I'm certain you could rattle off at least five people who have this belief that they've been slighted by someone. That slight affects their life. Even if the offense were real, why do these people waste so much of their energy trying to get even? Is there really a way to get even? Does the Lord want you to attack those who attack you? And what if they really didn't mean to offend you? Who's to say it wasn't the way you perceived it?

The fact is you were created to be better than always seeking revenge. You were created by an all-knowing, all-powerful Creator who loves you unconditionally. He put within you the propensity and ability to be creative and design amazing things. You were created to be not only a problem-solver but also a "tolerater." He put His peace within you to help in troubling times. But if you allow the spirit of offense to take hold of you, how will there be any room for you to house that creative Holy Spirit of God's? God gave you the power to overcome. Study your enemy so that you can learn how to defeat his attacks against you.

Be an overcomer instead of being overcome.

Be not overcome of evil, but overcome evil with good. (Rom. 12:21)

How would you like to be the coach of a local high school football team and practice, thinking that you are playing another high school from across town only to show up Friday night to find out you are playing the New England Patriots and Tom Brady? You would be shocked because you weren't prepared to face an opponent at that level.

THE TOXIC SPIRIT OF OFFENSE

You need to realize you have a spiritual opponent who is always working to take you down. One such entity of that opponent is the spirit of offense that we have been learning about. Peter calls the head of this enemy, the devil, a roaring lion who's seeking whom he may devour (1 Pet. 5:8). He wants to devour your home, your future, and all your opportunities. That is why God commands us, *"Be not overcome of evil..."* The devil and all of his spirits are evil, and you cannot let him overcome what God is doing in your life. Remember, *"If God be for us, who can be against us?" (Rom. 8:31).* Don't be overcome with his lies today. You cannot allow the temptation or tricks of the enemy to get the best of you. The God within you is more powerful than any temptation around you, so step into that authority and rise up as the man or woman of God you are. Overcome evil with good . . . because God is good. So trust God to give you the strength to overcome what you are facing today.

I believe that when we learn to deal with a spirit of offense, we learn to expel this offense out of our hearts. We can refuse to harbor those ill feelings toward another person. Through the power of God we will see an incredible spirit of creativity flow out of us with ideas that we never knew we could have. Ideas on how to increase our finances, how to be better husbands and wives, and even ideas on how to get promoted in life. The only reason those ideas are coming out is we got rid of what was blocking the flow: the spirit of offense.

The spirit of offense has the sole purpose of attaching itself to us in order to entangle us and stop the creative flow of God's Spirit within us. I want to show you the strategies the spirit of offense will use to attach itself to you with the intention of stopping the divine creative flow within you. The following information was taken from an online article by Ryan Johnson from *Charisma News* called "Prophetic Vision: The Spirit of Offense Wants to Attack You in These 8 Ways."

THE TOXIC SPIRIT OF OFFENSE

Strategy #1: The Spirit of Offense Will Attach to Your Mind

For God hath not given us the spirit of fear; but of power, and of love, and of a sound mind. (2 Tim. 1:7)

For they that are after the flesh do mind the things of the flesh; but they that are after the Spirit the things of the Spirit. For to be carnally minded is death; but to be spiritually minded is life and peace. (Rom. 8:5-6)

The spirit of offense will go after your mind first. If the devil and his team can get you into thinking carnally instead of spiritually, he has already won the battle. He knows you will lose the life and peace God wants you to have. Every battle is waged in the mind way before it is carried out.

Look at the passage in Romans again. Spiritual mindedness is what brings to your life peace from God. But when you are offended, that life and peace are interrupted because all you can do is think about what that person has said or done to you. Your mind has so much capacity to hold thoughts. And if those thoughts are toxic thoughts about what has happened to you in life, the creative thoughts you should have are pushed out and taken over by the thoughts of toxicity from the enemy.

I want to give you an example of toxic thoughts. For you men out there, this example almost always applies. Have you ever been in a fight with someone, perhaps in school or even later in life? After the fight you rarely think of the better way that you could have handled the situation leading up to the fight. Seldom are the moments when you put yourself in the other person's shoes and think about how he felt and how you could have defused the situation. No, most of the time later that day or lying down at night, we roll the film of the fight back through our minds, thinking of what or how we could have done it better. We scrutinize every aspect of the rumble—what we should have done, not done, and so forth. For hours or even days, sometimes years later we evaluate and revaluate that encounter trying to learn what we should have done better. We are more focused on how we performed during the toxic moment, rather than on not even having it—avoiding it altogether.

What we should have been thinking about was how that evil situation could have been totally avoided. The right thing would be to focus on the spiritual aspect, our righteous thoughts, but that's often not the case at all. It's many times not glamorous enough to relive the moments that end with humility. It's because the enemy needles our pride and tells us we are less than what we are. He tricks us into believing lies.

We are created to be creative, not to get even with people, not to worry about being offended. Yet when a spirit of offense gets into your mind, all you can think about is how to get even with the person whom it came from. Your imagination gets out of control, and you begin to imagine things about that person that may not even be true. This is what the Bible teaches us:

> *Casting down imaginations, and every high thing that exalteth itself against the knowledge of God, and bringing into captivity every thought to the obedience of Christ... (2 Cor. 10:5)*

The word *imagination* comes from the Greek *logismos*, which means a reckoning, computation. When you compute numerical figures, you come to a conclusion or an answer. When you compute 5+5, you come to the conclusion of 10 as the answer. When you compute 7x7, you come to the conclusion of 49 as the answer. The computation always lead you to a conclusion. Just like a mathematical computation adds things to a conclusion, so your imagination adds things to what is going on, and you come to a conclusion that is usually not accurate.

There are conclusions we have about other people based on the thoughts that we have about them in our minds. There are conclusions we have about ourselves now based on what has been said to us because the spirit of offense has caused us to imagine things about ourselves that are flat out not true.

Someone makes an offhanded comment about our appearance, and the spirit of offense gets ahold of us. It grabs our imagination leaving us contemplating if we are ugly or unlovable. It's a seed of doubt that if left to grow may blossom fully into a believed truth. After all, people do sometimes come to believe that awful things said about them are true. However, many people are sinful, and they do make sinful choices that hurt other people without demonic influence. Therefore, be careful about creating a demonic monster when it might just be a person who is in a foul mood and says something hurtful quite *on his or her own.*

Or maybe someone criticizes our work one day. Then that notion leads us to imagine whether what we do is really insufficient. Before we know it, if we do not correct that notion, we wonder every time we are working if we are doing a good job.

Do you see how this works? The spirit of offense is trying to take over your mind because the enemy knows what you are capable of doing. If he can sabotage the plans God has for your life, he has created yet another way to get you off of the path you should be traveling. Once confusion or hesitation is in your head, the smallest word spoken by someone might destroy all the hard work you have put into your life. You must not let this happen.

Strategy #2: The Spirit of Offense Will Attach to Your Sight

What you think about often determines what you see. Your mindset determines your sight. It's so true! If you want to test this theory, I have an experiment for you. Think of a car you don't normally recognize. Don't use a new Cadillac Escalade or anything like that but something that might be kind of rare. Let's use a Lamborghini. I bet if you were to think about it, you haven't seen a new one riding through town. But if you start looking for them, actually scanning parking lots and roads on your way to places, I bet you'll soon start seeing a few here and there. In fact, I bet you'll start seeing them in movies, TV shows, magazines, and everywhere else.

Is it magic that causes this to happen? Have you conjured up all these new cars? No. It's the power of suggestion and awareness. It's the phenomenon that what we focus our attention on seems to appear. It's all because we focus on something, so we notice it. It appears because we are looking for it. It has always been there. We just haven't known it was there. What you think about determines what you see. We then need to visualize what we want, but I'll get into that later. For now let's stay the course about your thought life.

What a person thinks about is so important. The Bible says in Proverbs 23:7:

For as he thinketh in his heart, so is he. (KJV)

Note how newer translations have stated it:

. . . for he is like one who is inwardly calculating. "Eat and drink!" he says to you, but his heart is not with you. (ESV)

. . . for he is the kind of person who is always thinking about the cost. "Eat and drink," he says to you, but his heart is not with you. (NIV)

THE TOXIC SPIRIT OF OFFENSE

Solomon here is warning us about the man who is the kind of person who is always *thinking* about the cost. "Eat and drink," he says to you, pretending to be a gracious host, but his heart is not with you—he's calculating every bite you eat and getting angrier as you continue to eat. He professes to be kind and generous, but it is not sincere; he is begrudging every bite of the food you eat, even though he has set it before you. He is a hypocrite first by his thoughts, then he is not what his *mouth* declares him to be. He says, "Eat and drink," but he is not happy when you enjoy yourself.

The KJV translation simply means that what is going on in his *heart* defines the man, not the profession of his mouth.

The spirit of offense will cause us to be blinded to all the great things God is doing in our lives. When the spirit of offense has attached itself to our vision, we begin to see the things that are not real, things that are not there. We see things as though they are something they are not.

Being under the attack of this spirit leaves you feeling like every post on social media is a direct attack against you. Every action, even someone looking at you, is perceived as an assault against you. What at one time had been seen as a generalized statement toward you now feels like fiery darts.

The spirit of offense will shift your vision from focusing on Godly purposes into trying to defend yourself against every onslaught seemingly headed your way. You should not be wasting your time and efforts against such things. You have too much in front of you to waste time worrying about what someone is or isn't saying about you. Your future is too precious to waste energy worrying about what another person thinks about you. It's imperative that you shake free from any toxic spirit accosting you, and to see God's plan for your future, you must be focused on Him.

Strategy #3: The Spirit of Offense Will Attach Itself to Your Heart

When you allow the spirit of offense to attach itself to your heart, everything you do, everything you say becomes toxic. Now I am not suggesting that every time this happens, the act is demonic. People can and do often choose to do or say things of their own volition that are simply downright evil. I know that sounds like an extreme statement, but when you consider the Biblical truth that out of our hearts come all the issues of life, then you understand how powerful the following Scripture is.

Keep thy heart with all diligence; for out of it are the issues of life. (Prov. 4:23)

The Lord echoes this statement.

"You brood of vipers! How can you speak good, when you are evil? For out of the abundance of the heart the mouth speaks." (Matt. 12:34b ESV)

Of course, some people are just sinful, and they are quite capable of making sinful choices that hurt other people without any demonic influence. However, some people have and do allow the spirit of offense to attach itself to their hearts; thus, they begin to speak bitter words to others. Their words become the emotional missiles launched at anyone who is within striking distance. They find themselves saying things they normally wouldn't say or doing things they normally wouldn't do. It's because the spirit of offense has penetrated their hearts and affected the most vital parts of their lives. Then these words become wounds, which create spiritual handicaps. If and when this happens, I would strongly suggest that everyone follow Paul's instruction in Ephesians 6 about combating spiritual forces.

The reason people are affected by the spirit of offense is] hurting people hurt others, which leads us to the fourth strategy.

Strategy #4: The Spirit of Offense Will Attach Itself to Your Relationships

One of the most tragic things I see with those afflicted by the spirit of offense is that they too often destroy their once-positive relationships. The spirit of offense will drive a wedge between a person and the relationships most needed in their life. That wedge will go anywhere: between family members, friend, or anyone else. Scripture explains why.

> *Whoever covers an offense seeks love, but he who repeats a matter separates close friends. (Prov. 17:9 ESV)*

When you're offended, you will seek people to tell them your side of the story in an attempt to get them on your side. You'll tend to repeat yourself and go over the scenario again and again to all who will listen. Doing this often drives a wedge between the people involved. It's all done consciously or not to drive a wedge between that person(s) you are telling the story to and the person who offended you. Go ahead and do this within your family, then see how Thanksgiving dinner goes that year.

God forbid that the people you complain to do not see it your way. This might be the quickest way to ruin friendships or outright lose them. You must use caution when dealing with this kind of spirit because its sole purpose is to destroy your connections with other people just like the entity it came from. It comes to kill, steal, and destroy.

THE TOXIC SPIRIT OF OFFENSE

Strategy #5: The Spirit of Offense Will Attach Itself to Your Hearing

Wherefore, my beloved brethren, let every man be swift to hear, slow to speak, slow to wrath ... (James 1:19)

Can you think back to the last time you were offended? Do you remember hearing many of the words spoken by the person who offended you *after* they offended you? The chances are slim that you heard everything the person said to you because it is a natural reaction to shut down our sensory organs. Many times it's an involuntary reaction. We think we are hearing them but really, we're lucky to be getting half of what they say.

When you are offended, you are not willing to hear what anyone else has to say. The offense has become so large at this point that what others say to you doesn't matter anymore because you are convinced they don't understand how hurt you feel. Because of this feeling, you refuse to listen to any counsel or any wisdom someone may try to bring to you that would deliver you from the spirit of offense that is attacking you.

The way of fools seems right to them, but the wise listen to advice. (Prov. 12:15 NIV)

The worst reaction we can have and is usually the response brought about by the spirit of offense is that we close our spiritual ears to everyone—including God. He tries to console us and put some wisdom in us. Regrettably, we are reveling in our anger and often want to be shut off from everything.

Instead of hearing His truth, our ears become tuned to the lies, manipulation, and deception of the enemy. Then we cannot hear the voice of God. We will spend the rest of our lives floundering without any direction.

Go back to that passage in the book of James.

Wherefore, my beloved brethren, let every man be swift to hear, slow to speak, slow to wrath ... (James 1:19)

Imagine the opposite of that verse. What if we were slow to hear? Wouldn't that mean we would be swift to speak and swift to wrath? Sounds like the people who refuse to listen end up in the most arguments with others.

Strategy #6: The Spirit of Offense Will Attach Itself to Your Physical Health

Our relationships with others, as well as the spirits that influence our lives, directly affect our natural bodies, our strength, and our vitality. The spirit of offense affects our health in general.

Wherefore, my beloved brethren, let every man be swift to hear, slow to speak, slow to wrath ... (James 1:19)

Several years ago I remember reading about a national study regarding people who hold grudges. A researcher questioned nearly 10,000 U.S. residents asking them, "Would you say this is true or false? I've held grudges against people for years."

Slightly more than 6,500 people responded yes to the question.

The researchers reported that those who said they did indeed hold grudges were found to be far less healthy. Among those 6,500 people, a higher rate of heart disease, cardiac arrest, elevated blood pressure, stomach ulcers, back problems, headaches, and chronic pain were found. Those who did not answer yes had significantly lower rates of health problems.

The spirit of offense and its teammates has one purpose, and that purpose is to destroy you. According to this research it appears that they may cause health problems that could outright kill you.

THE TOXIC SPIRIT OF OFFENSE

The spirit of offense comes directly from the enemy. Its purpose is to tear you away from God's good example and end your life away from Him. Being aware of the spirit and understanding its goal is imperative to taking the steps to avoid allowing this toxin into your life. There is a fight being waged around you and probably within your life. What way will you handle it? Will you ho-hum it and expect everything to be just fine without due diligence? Or will you be on guard, protecting your life from the spirit of offense? Remember that our Father expects you to be prepared.

> *Keep thy heart with all diligence; for out of it are the issues of life. (Prov. 4:23)*

Guard your heart, guard your mind, and keep your spirit before the throne of God. When you feel offense knocking at your door, go directly to the person involved in the offense and take care of it immediately. I have always noticed that iron bends easiest while it's still hot.

Recognize that a true brother who offends you or whom you offend will be eager to work out differences. They should want to remedy any issues. If they don't want to, well . . . were they really a brother or sister to begin with?

> *If your brother or sister sins, go and point out their fault, just between the two of you. If they listen to you, you have won them over. (Matt. 18:15 NIV)*

CHAPTER 6

How to Deal With the Spirit of Offense

The fact that this world of ours is so saturated and possessed by the spirit of offense and his teammates tells me that more information and attention are needed on the subject. You have already heard a good deal of information about how this evil and intrusive spirit's goal is to poison our lives.

Now in this chapter I'll give you some ways to respond to this spirit, to combat it. It is such a prevalent spirit in today's world that everyone needs to learn how to repel it. And doing so will allow you to live a more joyful life.

There is an art to living a life that's free from the care of being offended. Stop for a moment and think about how great life would be if you could live each day without being offended. Can you imagine how beautiful it would be to live a life where you could listen to the radio, watch the news, and get through a full workday and not have a single person or topic offend you? Can you imagine how low your level of stress and anxiety would be if you could live above what you think people are saying or thinking about you? What would it be like to live life at a level where you don't worry when someone else does something better than you or when you don't think the worst when someone you know walks by you without acknowledging you? I can all but guarantee that your life will be much happier, and you will be much healthier when you can master the art of living the offense-free life.

I don't just believe this kind of life is possible, I know it's the will of God for us to live life at a level far above being offended. The Lord Jesus instructs us in Matthew 18:15, *"If your brother sins against you, go and tell him his fault, between you and him alone" (ESV).* Why didn't he say, "Just live 'above being offended'; get over it?"

It is certainly true that there are offenses that I can overlook, as Solomon wrote in Proverbs 19:11 and we definitely should; however, that is not the whole story. There are offenses so serious and sinful that cause a breach in relationships. We are not to overlook those but follow Jesus' counsel in Matthew 18.

> *Good sense makes one slow to anger, and it is his glory to overlook an offense. (Prov. 19:11 ESV)*

It makes "good sense"—according to the Lord's Word—to be slow to anger and overlook an offense. Our Lord wants us to live a life where we can forgive quickly and give abundantly.

> *"But I say unto you, That ye resist not evil: but whosoever shall smite thee on thy right cheek, turn to him the other also. And if any man will sue thee at the law, and take away thy coat, let him have thy cloak also. And whosoever shall compel thee to go a mile, go with him twain." (Matt. 5:39-41)*

Think about this. Most people offend you because they love to see your reaction when you get upset. So what would happen if you quit giving them that response they are looking for? What do you think they would do if you took away their favorable response? There would be no reward for them. No satisfaction to be gained through the process. What would happen if you showed them that God's grace in your life was more powerful than the hurtful words that came out of their mouths or the division that they are trying to create through circumstances? What if you showed them that you were the bigger person and that their juvenile attempts meant nothing to you?

I'll tell you exactly what would happen. That person, that spirit of offense, would move on to a more willing participant. And that, my friend, is the earmark of spiritual maturity. When people can do or say something that used to offend you but you have instead chosen to take the high road and pay back hate with the love of Christ, that is spiritual growth at its finest. Paul's words express the mindset you want to develop.

> *Recompense to no man evil for evil. Provide things honest in the sight of all men. If it be possible, as much as lieth in you, live peaceably with all men. (Rom. 12:17-18)*

The key verse in this Scripture is, *"As much as lieth in you."* It means, you are not responsible for what other people say or do; you are responsible only for how you respond to it.

> *Submit yourselves therefore to God. Resist the devil, and he will flee from you. (James 4:7)*

There are many things that can poison your heart. Some people struggle with an outward temptation of alcohol, sexual sin, or toxic relationships. Still others battle with an inward temptation of jealousy, bitterness, lust, fantasies, or some form of emotional sin like the spirit of offense. It really doesn't matter what it is that you struggle with; it all comes from a single source, which is the enemy of our soul. The devil is out to *"kill, steal, and destroy" (John 10:10)*, and he doesn't care how he does it. He will come subtly at you with issues intended to disable you from pursuing the life God wants you to live and disarm your spiritual success.

That's why James gives us this formula in James 4:7: *"Submit yourselves to God. Resist the devil and he will flee from you."* It's as simple as that. When you have submitted your life to Christ, you have the authority to resist the devil, and he has no choice but to flee from you. You cannot entertain his temptation even for a moment. You must resist it. Even one moment of consideration about indulging that temptation may lead you down the road to compromise and will often cause you to do the very thing the devil wants to use to destroy you. So get up today and use that authority you have been given. Understand that the choice is yours. You do not have to follow the devil and his ways just because so much of the world does. Because of Christ, the choice of how you react to each situation is completely up to you. Following your Savior means you can be victorious over the enemy's schemes.

Think hard about what has just been said. This principle is an important one—one you have been taught over and over throughout your life. Be responsible for how you react. Responsibility is your ability to respond. If you are going to exercise responsibility, that means you exercise your ability to respond in a way that you see as justifiable or correct. You must make the choice: do you follow the status quo of this world and allow others to dictate the direction of your life, the stability of your emotions? Do you get upset with a person when they gossip about you? Do you lash out at one who criticizes your ways or your faith?

If you get bent out of shape over what someone says about you or to you, then you are giving that person control over your emotions. When you react to what other people say or do to you, you become a prisoner of their poison. You give them the key to unlock the door to your emotions. Pay attention to this nugget of truth because it's 100 percent real. If you can incorporate this fact into your life, I guarantee you'll be able to gain more control over the spirit of offense.

The more offended you become,

The more people will offend you.

It's so very true. It's like adding oxygen to a fire. It's going to grow larger and larger until it's out of your control. As long as you let it control you, it will. You must busy yourself in Scripture. Every answer, every solution is there for your benefit.

> *All things are lawful unto me, but all things are not expedient: all things are lawful for me, but I will not be brought under the power of any. (1 Cor. 6:12)*

Recognize that our Lord Jesus Christ died a horrific death so that we no longer are slaves to sin. Without Him, we are the walking dead. But because of what He did for us, all things changed. We were handed the keys to the Kingdom (Matt. 16:19) and given the power to overcome all this world has to offend us with.

Now I'd like to give you three principles that, if used, will change your life. These realizations will help defend you against the spirit of offense.

Principle #1: Be Intentional About Who You Are

> *For you created my inmost being; you knit me together in my mother's womb. I praise you because I am fearfully and wonderfully made; your works are wonderful, I know that full well. (Ps. 139:13-14 NIV)*

> *For we are God's handiwork, created in Christ Jesus to do good works, which God prepared in advance for us to do. (Eph. 2:10 NIV)*

Decide what it is you want. I imagine because you are reading this book, you want to be more like Christ. Or you at least don't want the devil in your life. Since you are feeling that way, I need you to understand that being secure in Christ is the first step to living a life that's free from offense.

This is where most people stumble on their voyage with offense. They are not secure in who they are, which explains why when people speak ill about them or accost them with accusations, it seems to hurt them so much. It's a sad reality that we care so deeply about what others say about us.

I feel strongly about the facts I'm putting to you right now. I know that so many people out there are having their lives directed by the choices of others. They are not making their own choices. Because of this, they find themselves living a life that isn't true to who God has created them to be. They are not following the plans God created for them.

> *"For I know the plans I have for you," declares the* LORD, *"plans to prosper you and not to harm you, plans to give you hope and a future. Then you will call on me and come and pray to me, and I will listen to you. You will seek me and find me when you seek me with all your heart." (Jer. 29:11-13 NIV)*

You get one shot at this life, so you better make it count. You need to make sure you are not living your life by what other people think or say you should be doing. They won't be the ones who will have to give an answer for you on the Day of Judgment. No excuse involving someone else is going to cause Jesus to give you a pass. *You* are in control of your life, which means you better learn to take responsibility for your actions now. It's time for you to take the reins of your life. It is time to live an intentional life.

One of the biggest reasons people do not live an intentional life is they are too busy living the life others expect them to live. They spend their entire lives allowing someone else to make their most important decisions for them. It amazes me that so many people will follow what's happening on social media and let that dictate what happens in their lives. They allow the persuasive voice of people around them to silence the voice of the Holy Spirit within them.

Intentional living is the art of making your own choices before the choices others make of you. It's time that you take control of the decisions in your life. Your decisions and all of the repercussions are going to fall on you. You might as well start accepting responsibility now. You're going to face the music one day and answer for the direction your life took. Do not try to avoid any of it now. This journey of life is short. The older you get, the more you realize just how short it really is.

> ... yet you do not know what tomorrow will bring. What is your life? For you are a mist that appears for a little time and then vanishes. (James 4:14 ESV)

The one thing you don't want to happen on this journey is to simply become a passenger being driven by someone else's dreams. You need to be the driver on this journey with your GPS set to the God-given purpose assigned to you. Be intentional about who you are.

The key is to focus on God and forego the worries of the world. The more you focus on who God has created you to be, the less you'll worry about what others are trying to recreate you to be.

You should get up every morning and thank God for who you are. Thank Him for the gifts and abilities He has placed within you. Thank Him for your physical appearance. Thank Him because you are thoughtfully and carefully made. Believe that who He made you to be is going to work out for your benefit in the end. The first key to living an unoffended life is to be intentional about who you are and find your security in Christ alone.

Principle #2: Be Intentional About Where You Are Going

Brothers and sisters, I do not consider myself yet to have taken hold of it. But one thing I do: Forgetting what is behind and straining toward what is ahead, I press on toward the goal to win the prize for which God has called me heavenward in Christ Jesus. (Phil. 3:13-14 NIV)

The Apostle Paul is an example we should definitely look toward because he's one of the most focused individuals of the Bible. I believe it's because he was intentional about where he was going, which meant he refused to allow anything to distract him from getting there.

And now, behold, I go bound in the spirit unto Jerusalem, not knowing the things that shall befall me there: Save that the Holy Ghost witnesseth in every city, saying that bonds and afflictions abide me. But none of these things move me, neither count I my life dear unto myself, so that I might finish my course with joy, and the ministry, which I have received of the Lord Jesus, to testify the gospel of the grace of God. (Acts 20:22-24)

Paul was saying that he didn't know what was going to happen to him when he got to Jerusalem. He didn't know what the people were going to say or do to him.

Paul knew that his agenda, his God-given and God-guided agenda, was much more important than what others wanted him to do. He knew that his destination was so much bigger than what people said about him or did to him. He had this resolute belief that he was not going to allow someone other than God to move him off of the path he was meant to walk.

Nay, in all these things we are more than conquerors through him that loved us. For I am persuaded, that neither death, nor life, nor angels, nor principalities, nor powers, nor things present, nor things to come, Nor height, nor depth, nor any other creature, shall be able to separate us from the love of God, which is in Christ Jesus our Lord. (Rom. 8:37-39)

Just like Paul, your path in life is set by God. And like him it's too important for you to allow what people do or say to derail you from your God-given destination. What God is doing in your life right now is too precious for you to allow what other people say to take away the power of what He is doing within you. Don't let it happen!

You have to get into sync with the plans God has for your life. Begin by writing out some of the goals you have for your life. Focus your prayer time on the will of God. He has a purpose for you. Try to determine what that is and how you'll achieve it. Get a vision about the life God set aside for you. Picture it in your head and lay out its scenarios daily.

Being laser-focused on the destination of your life means you will be less focused on its distractions. Getting offended is to allow toxins in that are distractions from where God wants you to go. Getting offended is a detour from the path you are meant to follow. Nothing is more important than your living out the purpose for which you were created.

Do not be content to become a backseat passenger to someone else's desires for your life. Imagine this scenario. You want to go on vacation. It's just you, and your heart is set on Paris. You get online and do a little research. After a bit you find the deal you want and handle all the details. The day comes when you head to the airport. You walk up to the person with a smiling face behind the counter to pick up your prepaid ticket. When he hands it to you, that's when you notice the destination is Mumbai, India.

"There has been a mistake," you say. "I'm scheduled for Paris, France."

To your amazement you hear the man explain, "Yes, sir, we saw that. But we believe you would have more fun in Mumbai, India."

That's not how it works. You would never let an airline agent determine your destination. Yet so many times in your life you have allowed others to change your path. Why?

You must not let other people's ideas or their thoughts drive you. And you better not let other people's criticisms change you. It's time for you to be intentional about both who you are and where you're going. When you are sure of who you are and where you're going, the mindless opinions of others really don't matter to you anymore.

Principle #3: Don't Take Yourself Too Seriously

"I am come that they might have life, and that they might have it more abundantly." (John 10:10b)

Jesus didn't say that He came so we could "make a living." He came so that we could live a life, and not just any old life, but an *abundant one.* I think we sometimes forget that.

God gave us the gift of life so that it could be enjoyed, not endured. Life is a gift. Imagine if you just put in a bunch of overtime so you could buy your spouse that perfect car they've wanted their entire life. And then after they got it, they parked it in the garage, never drove it, and took the bus. What a waste of a gift, right? God has given us this gift of life. And the worst thing is that far too many people won't use it for its original purpose. They walk through it simply dealing with whatever comes their way or affects them.

We need to live our lives abundantly. Live a life that's full of love, joy, and laughter.

> *Nehemiah said, "Go and enjoy choice food and sweet drinks, and send some to those who have nothing prepared. This day is holy to our Lord. Do not grieve, for the joy of the LORD is your strength." (Neh. 8:10 NIV)*

If we intentionally live with the joy that God intended for us to have, we would be less concerned about what others say or think about us. What happens when you ask a group of kids to draw? They start drawing. What if you asked them to dance? They just dance. But what if you asked a group of adults to do the same things? Most of them would probably ask "Why?" or just say "No."

Why is that? What's the difference between when we are young or older? I'll tell you. When we get older, we use our logic-based reasoning to decide most things. Our lives and choices are jaded by past examples of ridicule and embarrassment, which means we immediately wonder if someone is trying to embarrass us or use us. Why are we so afraid of embarrassment? It's because we have created an image within ourselves that's unrealistic. I believe that God wants us to enjoy the life we have been given and not worry about the expectations of the people around us.

> *"If you, then, though you are evil, know how to give good gifts to your children, how much more will your Father in heaven give good gifts to those who ask him!" (Matt. 7:11 NIV)*

Part of the problem with being so offended is that we don't know how to laugh at ourselves. We need to develop the ability to own up to our mistakes and not be so critical of ourselves. Being comfortable in our own skin makes people more comfortable around us. There are some simple measures you can take so as to not take yourself so seriously.

First: Stop Trying to Please Everyone

Am I now trying to win the approval of human beings, or of God? Or am I trying to please people? If I were still trying to please people, I would not be a servant of Christ. (Gal. 1:10 NIV)

The problem with trying to please everyone is that usually you are left as the person who's the most unhappy. Centering your life on the approval of the people in this world means you will eventually die from their rejection. People really don't think about you as much as you think they do. Lighten up. Stop trying to make everyone happy—you can't.

Second: Realize You Are Human Just Like Everyone Else

We all stumble in many ways. Anyone who is never at fault in what they say is perfect, able to keep their whole body in check. (James 3:2 NIV)

I believe that many people who take themselves too seriously think they are the only ones who have it all together. Trust me: no one has it all together. All people are flawed. When you realize that the people you fear the most are just people too, it will change the way you approach them. You will be more confident and harder to offend.

Third: Remove Sources of Negativity

But avoid foolish controversies and genealogies and arguments and quarrels about the law, because these are unprofitable and useless. Warn a divisive person once, and then warn them a second time. After that, have nothing to do with them. You may be sure that such people are warped and sinful; they are self-condemned. (Tit. 3:9-11 NIV)

If you know you have a problem with something, say . . . alcohol, why then would you go to work at a bar, eat in a tavern, and hang out with your alcoholic friends? Sometimes the most logical thing is to remove yourself from negative situations and remove the sources that offend you the most.

CHAPTER 7

He's the Protector Against Toxicity

We have been trying to absorb the fact thus far that the world can be a very poisonous place filled with pitfalls set by the devil in order to make us stumble. There have been discussions regarding toxic relationships, victim mentality, and even information given on evil spirits that attack and oppress us. What we have yet to discuss at length is that there is given to us a great shield of protection. That shield is Almighty God Himself. Jesus Christ is our Savior in all ways, against all things. This, of course, includes all toxicity found in this world. We must learn to utilize this protection in our lives.

The Lord Jesus Christ is the protector against toxicity. It is through Him that all men might believe in the Father (John 1:7). It's through Him that the world is saved (John 3:17). And we are also given eternal life through Him (John 20:31). So you see, everything is possible *through* Jesus.

In the previous chapters we have discussed how, at times, we just don't take enough responsibility for ourselves. We have to take more control over our lives. This chapter is different. Here I have some new advice for you.

To find protection and healing from every manner of toxin, you need to let go of the reins and give control over to God.

Yes. You have that right. Do less.

Notice that I *did not* say do nothing. To have the fervent support of God in your life, you cannot ever do nothing. There is an important element of action that is at play even with faith. There's a need for you to pray, and the great thing is that the Bible teaches us how to do that.

I love flying, but I hate turbulence. I believe all of us have been on bumpy flights where seemingly out of nowhere the smooth ride is turned suddenly to one where you are tossed about so violently that you wonder if you'll ever see solid ground again. There are ups, downs, and twists that leave you reeling.

The reality is that life is many times like a plane flying through turbulent skies. You take off with high aspirations of what you'll become and where you'll go. You find yourself flying higher and higher. You see the clear blue skies as you are climbing. Then just when you get to cruising altitude, you hit a patch of clouds that cause some serious turbulence. You're never fully prepared for the twists and turns that turbulence brings. The only thing you can do is grab hold of something solid and hold on for dear life. The more twists and turns that come your way, the tighter you hold on.

That is exactly the way life is many times. We seem to be climbing the ladder of success. Things are going well. We have a goal set, and we aim to reach it. It's a great goal, too. One that will please God and do a little something for us.

Then suddenly something happens, and we feel ourselves plummeting downward. And as if that downfall weren't bad enough, then come the twists and turns. It's bad enough that we feel our demise coming, but now we have to be sick on our way to it. The worst part is the unknown. We don't know exactly what's coming next. The only thing we know to do for sure is hold on tight.

Do you know what you better be holding on to? It's Jesus. But a major problem with so many people is that they lose faith in the face of turbulence. Yes, most of them are crying out for His help, but so much of it is only in lip service. They are not strong in their faith because so much toxicity has grabbed hold of their lives.

Perhaps the most toxic thought people can have is when they plan their own lives and "use" Christ only as a life preserver. Or worse, they don't seek Him at all. Some of you are dangerously close to doing that right now. You find yourselves falling and are grasping for anything solid. Anything at all. This is a dangerous time.

You must be careful during the trying times of your life. The devil is a crafty creature who will cause the turmoil in your life in hopes that in your desperation you will reach out for his help to save you. Obviously, you don't know it's him that you are grabbing hold of. You think it's a friend, family member, or even a substance that is getting you through some tough spots, but it's nothing of the sort. Anytime you reach out to anything other than the Lord Jesus for guidance in your life, you are reaching for the wrong thing. You must look for the answers to your problems using all that is spiritual. Regrettably, too many lean on their soulish man.

Difficult times in life lead us to respond out of our soulish man rather than our spiritual man. We say or do something out of our emotions rather than our spirits. Too often these are not the right things.

So what is your soul? The human soul is the human self or personality. The Greek word *psuche* is the source of the English word "soul" from which we derive the words "psychology," "psychiatry," and "psychoanalysis."

HE'S THE PROTECTOR AGAINST TOXICITY

The human soul is the human psyche, which is made up of three elements:

Intellect: has to do with a man's mind, thoughts, and wisdom.

Emotions: his moods, desires, ideals, loves, likes, dislikes, hates, sorrows, and joys; the total feeling of mankind.

Volition: man's willpower, the exercise of his will as in making a deliberate decision or choice.

It's from the human soul that man thinks, feels, and decides.

I'll tell you that the majority of the battles you will face will be fought in the realm of the human soul. It's because the enemy is going to fight you using your own emotions, thoughts, and feelings against you. He knows that if he can control what's in your head, then he can control what's in your heart.

The enemy wants to control what you are doing. To do that he must try to control what you do—to control what you are doing with your hands. If you are looking toward God for help, understand that He cannot change what's in your hand until He changes what's in your head. You have to give God control of your soulish man. This is why it's so important to continually come back to the Word of God when we are facing these emotional struggles and battles because it's the Word of God that feeds the spirit man.

The Word of God does not feed the soulish man. In fact, it is the Word of God that separates the soulish man from the spiritual man.

For the word of God is living and active, sharper than any two-edged sword, piercing to the division of soul and of spirit, of joints and of marrow, and discerning the thoughts and intentions of the heart. (Heb. 4:12 ESV; emphasis added)

An argument often made in reference to Hebrews 4:12 is also this: <u>since</u> this passage uses different words to describe the essence of man's nature, <u>then</u> they must be *distinctly different parts.*

In light of the weight of the Scriptural evidence that I have provided you with earlier in a previous chapter, showing that soul and spirit are also used interchangeably and are referring to the totality of the immaterial aspect of man, then this passage, too, could be seen as using these synonyms for emphasis. It is as if someone would encourage you to fight with all of your strength and all of your might. Strength = might; the two are used for emphasis.

Rather than looking at the passage as listing six individual parts of the human person: spirit, soul, joints, marrow, thoughts, and attitudes, one might look at the passage as listing <u>two</u> things that the Word of God can penetrate and divide: *the spiritual part of man* (soul/spirit) and *the physical part of man* (joints/marrow); followed by an action: judging the heart (thoughts/attitudes).

This can also be a correct way to view the passage. Don't you just love theology? The author of Hebrews **does not say** that the Word of God divides "the soul *from* the spirit." He lists six items that refer to the deep inner parts of a person that *are not hidden* from the penetrating power of the Word of God. If we wish to think metaphorically of our inmost being as hidden in our joints and marrow, then God's power can pierce deeply even there! God's Word goes to the very depth of our being—however we describe it—to expose disobedience and lack of submission to His leadership in our lives.

Whatever is fed the most will become the strongest. Whatever is the strongest will win the battle.

There's no doubt that a war between good and evil is raging. Right? The devil is trying to separate us from our Creator at all costs, and God is trying to give us all we need to combat that evil and live eternally with Him in Heaven.

The choice, then, is up to us. Will we follow the narrow road to heaven? Or do we allow ourselves to be slowly poisoned by the multitude of toxins and toxic people the devil puts in our path? If your choice is heaven, then you're in the right book. And here is the key to getting assistance for your rise to bliss: Pray. Pray to God, and He will show you all, be all, and help you in all ways. Pray without ceasing. Pray for answers. Pray for direction. Just pray to God! And when you're done with that—pray some more.

The key to every great relationship is communication. It is the single most important element that will help two people understand one another. If you want help from God, then you need to talk to Him. He desperately wants to help you in every single way imaginable. And perhaps the greatest part is that His Holy Spirit can and often does guide you in what to say. When the disciples asked Jesus what they should say when speaking to the Father in heaven, He was not vague in the answer. He spoke clearly. He said plainly,

> *"After this manner therefore pray ye: Our Father which art in heaven, Hallowed be thy name. Thy kingdom come, Thy will be done in earth, as it is in heaven. Give us this day our daily bread. And forgive us our debts, as we forgive our debtors. And lead us not into temptation, but deliver us from evil: For thine is the kingdom, and the power, and the glory, for ever. Amen." (Matt. 6:9-13)*

Jesus knew this was a perfect way to pray. In Psalm 23 God used the psalmist to announce His promise to His people, His promise to care and provide for those who followed Him. He loves us like no other and wants to provide like no other father does. He knew how prevalent the devil would be in man's life, and He knew we would need a way to avoid his toxicity. So the Father gave us a way to worship Him and gain strength over the evil one.

This well-known Psalm (23) is one of the best at addressing many spiritual aspects of the human experience. David was a worshiper. No matter what danger or what prosperous place he found himself in, David was always a worshiper. You read the Psalms and you can feel the passion in this man's heart. It's why no matter what he faced, he always went to God the Father in worship and prayer. He was favored by God because he always prayed.

In this particular Psalm, David addresses how God meets you at each level of your life and in every experience in your life. He shows you how to address God and gain protection and love from the greatest provider ever. David knew it, and you need to as well. Prayer gives you power to overcome. You want to know how to fight the devil? Pray to God. Here's how you do it.

Understanding #1: He is My Shepherd

The Lord is my shepherd; I shall not want. (Ps. 23:1)

In his book, *I Shall Not Want*, Robert Ketchum tells about a Sunday school teacher who asked her group of children if any of them could quote the entire twenty-third Psalm. A little five-year-old girl was among those who raised their hands. A bit skeptical, the teacher asked if she could really quote the entire psalm. The little girl came to the podium, faced the class, made a little bow and said, "The Lord is my shepherd, that's all I want." She may have overlooked a few verses, but I think that little girl captured David's heart in Psalm 23.

When you know who your shepherd is, there's nothing else in this world that you will ever need or even desire. David himself was a shepherd, so he was qualified to write what he did in this Psalm because after all, he knew from firsthand experience that the lot of any particular sheep depends on the type of man who owns it. Under one man, sheep might struggle, starve, or suffer endless hardships. But under another, they might flourish and thrive contentedly.

The level of comfort in the sheep is completely dependent on the level of competency in the shepherd. Jesus has chosen us. He has redeemed us. He has bought us by His shed blood. He has gone to great lengths to bring us into His flock. Knowing this, we can be sure that He is eager to protect us from the devil and any toxic thing of this world.

Don't you know that you must change your mindset? If you believe that people take care of you, then you're looking to the wrong savior. Jesus has chosen to take care of you. Your protection, prosperity, and providence do not rely on anyone or anything of this world. Your government doesn't take care of you. Your employer doesn't take care of you. Your Shepherd takes care of you! Put your faith and praise in Him, and you'll have nothing to worry about.

"I am the good shepherd: the good shepherd giveth his life for the sheep." (John 10:11)

The good Shepherd will <u>guard</u> the sheep. It's the utmost desire of a good shepherd to make certain his sheep are able to thrive. With so many wild animals that put the flock at risk every night, the shepherd is always on watch for that which may cause harm to his sheep. From sunrise to sunrise, 24/7, the shepherd is protecting and guiding. The Lord is the Shepherd, people. I'm not really talking about animals.

The eyes of the LORD are upon the righteous, and his ears are open unto their cry. (Ps. 34:15)

The righteous cry, and the LORD heareth, and delivereth them out of all their troubles. (Ps. 34:17)

Therefore will not we fear, though the earth be removed, and though the mountains be carried into the midst of the sea; Though the waters thereof roar and be troubled, though the mountains shake with the swelling thereof. Selah. (Ps. 46:2-3)

You have nothing to fear, for fear will paralyze you. You are protected from all the toxic things of this world when you allow the great Shepherd Jesus to call you a member of His flock. The devil, his evil spirits, immoral influential people, drugs, and alcohol, all of it can be gone when you rely on His protection.

A good shepherd will <u>guide</u> His sheep. We get so lost in wanting to control our lives that we forget we are supposed to be following. We make things so difficult when they could be so easy. We need to rely on Christ. Be convinced that our steps are being ordered by the Lord right now. Even though we might not understand where God is taking us, we have to have faith that it's exactly where we need to be.

You might be scared or maybe you are saturated by toxins and think there's no way for you to get out. If that's the case, then you need to trust in God more than the next man.

When my spirit faints within me, you know my way! In the path where I walk they have hidden a trap for me. (Ps. 142:3 ESV)

I cry to you, O LORD; I say, "You are my refuge, my portion in the land of the living." Attend to my cry, for I am brought very low! Deliver me from my persecutors, for they are too strong for me! Bring me out of prison, that I may give thanks to your name! The righteous will surround me, for you will deal bountifully with me. (Ps. 142:5-7 ESV)

You may feel like the psalmist, trapped in the dark like David in this cave. He thought that his enemies had laid snares everywhere for him, but he had faith that God would save him. He believed that God not only knew his path but also was the one who planned it out for him. Even when his heart was overwhelmed and he knew the entrapments of the enemy, David took solace that God had already planned out his path for the rest of his days and would take care of him.

You may be reading this right now and feeling as though you live your life running and hiding from your enemies. People have said things to you and about you that are like snares meant to entrap you. You may feel overwhelmed in your spirit like there's nothing you can do. But the one thing you must hold on to is this: God knows the path you are taking. He will guide every step you take as long as you trust Him and hold His hand. Even though you may emotionally feel as though you are in a dark cave in life right now, God knows right where you are. David praised the Lord, worshiped Him all the day long.

Understanding #2: He is My Supplier

He maketh me to lie down in green pastures: he leadeth me beside the still waters. (Ps. 23:2a)

For sheep to lie down, four things need to happen:

They must be free from all fear.

There must be no tension among members of the flock.

They must not be aggravated with flies or parasites.

They must be free from hunger.

The shepherd will do absolutely everything he can in his power to bring his sheep into a position where they are willing to lie down, receive rest, and have their needs met.

HE'S THE PROTECTOR AGAINST TOXICITY

Jesus wants to meet your needs. He understands that sometimes you will be under an attack. He knows everything about your life. He is waiting for you to concede power to Him. He wants to be the One who is supplying you with everything you need. He also wants to be the One delivering you from all that you don't want in your life: the negative and oppressive people, the backbiters and liars, and every other sort that brings anything toxic into your life can be diminished when you understand God's power that's available to you.

When a follower of Jesus is faithfully following him, that is often *the very time* when the Enemy attacks most ferociously. If you read the biographies of faithful men of God, you will hear that story again and again—incredible suffering, terrible opposition, real struggle—*because that individual is really standing for Jesus and the Kingdom!*

In Ephesians 6, Paul warns against the onslaught of the Enemy. He does not say that if you have *faith,* all the "negative and oppressive people, the backbiters and liars," and the demonic powers will *be gone.* What he does say is "take your stand" (v. 11) and concludes by writing, "stand firm then" (v. 14). The Greek verb means to make a stand, hold out against, or to hold one's ground. It has a military sense in this passage; it is an exhortation to the Christian soldier to hold his ground against the attack of the Enemy. If all opposition were simply gone at conversion, there would be no need to stand or to hold one's ground!

Telling the Lord that you believe in Him and that you know He's going to take care of it all isn't enough for Him. You have to have faith that He will take care of you as well.

I want to tell you today to stop worrying about your needs being met. Realize that God will bring you into the exact position you need to be in order for every one of your needs to be met. Because He's your divine Supplier, it is His nature to make certain that your needs are met. Putting your faith in Him while praising Him means that it's impossible for Him *not* to provide for you.

God may move you out from the pasture where you have been grazing into a better one, or He may lead you into close range of the wolf pack, but He will be there to strengthen you whatever you may face .

You have to be ready to listen. If you're praising the Lord and putting your faith in Him, then you had better be ready for an answer. This might mean that removing the toxic people and places of our life involves moving you. You have to be willing to do what He needs you to do. He's your supplier of all things. Sometimes that means a fresh start.

> *. . . he leadeth me beside the still waters. (Ps. 23:2b)*

Although sheep will not drink from fast-moving or turbulent waters, I'd direct your attention to passages like:

> *Indeed, all who desire to live a godly life in Christ Jesus will be persecuted, while evil people and impostors will go on from bad to worse, deceiving and being deceived. (2 Tim. 3:12-13 ESV)*

> *"If the world **hates you**, keep in mind that it hated me first. If you belonged to the world, it would love you as its own. As it is, you **do not belong** to the world, but I have chosen you out of the world. **That is why the world hates you** .. If they persecuted me, they will persecute you also." (John 15:18-19, 20b NIV; emphasis added)*

So Jesus taught that it is the will of God for you to suffer from time to time. He said, in fact, to *expect it.*

However, you do not have to continually suffer from spiritual turbulence. Nor does God expect you to be troubled by your environment. He knows you cannot be properly nourished by Him if you are suffering from unrest and turbulence within.

> *On the last and greatest day of the festival, Jesus stood and said in a loud voice, "Let anyone who is thirsty come to me and drink." (John 7:37 NIV)*

Understanding #3: He is My Sustainer

Yea, though I walk through the valley of the shadow of death, I will fear no evil: for thou art with me . . . (Ps. 23:4)

Someone reading these words right now is probably walking through some dark valleys. You are being overrun by demonic spirits that are slowly destroying who you want to be and who God created you to be. The toxins of this world: negativity, evil, hatred, obsession, and so much more are making you walk through a scary valley. You might be so engulfed in that evil that you are wondering if you will ever get out. No matter how hard you try, you simply seem stuck in that same dark, lonely place. You've been there so long that you're starting to forget the Sun.

David uses this picture as if to say, *It doesn't matter how dark the valley, I know that You God are with me. I have absolutely nothing to fear. Because in the time of my greatest need, You are going to sustain me and keep me going. Even when I can't see the light.*

And how does David know this? Because he knows the shepherd has a rod and a staff.

. . . thy rod and thy staff they comfort me. (Ps. 23:4b)

Both of these instruments will be what lead him out of the valley and back to the mountaintop where it seems that the Lord is easier to see and hear.

When a shepherd is out in the field with his flock, he carries very little with him. Today's shepherd will carry a rifle, a staff, and a knapsack. In the Middle East the shepherd carried only a rod and staff.

The rod is like a club. The shepherd learns from childhood how to throw it with amazing speed and accuracy. It becomes his main weapon of defense for himself and his sheep. He uses it to drive off predators like coyotes, wolves, cougars, or strays.

The staff, on the other hand, is a long, slender stick, often with a crook or hook on one end. The staff was not used for defense but rather for direction. God kind of does the same thing for us, doesn't He? He doesn't beat us over the head with His mighty club. He either allows certain circumstances to take place, or He puts people in our way to nudge us in the right direction. He shuts us off from those who might aim to hurt us. When we pray for His guidance, He'll do whatever He desires to answer us as long as it coincides with what He wants us to do.

I'm paraphrasing, but David basically was saying, *I know that no matter what enemies we will face while we walk through this valley, your rod will beat them away. If by chance we lose our way while in that valley, Your staff will bring us right back on course.*

The valley we live in can be dangerous not just because of the evil spirits that are all throughout the valley but also because of the temptations that grip our hearts. The flesh wants what it wants. Sometimes it seems hard to do the right thing. Why? Because we live in fear of all the evil around us or simply because the desires or lusts in our own hearts are opposed to God's will. Sometimes it's just because we want what we want.

We cannot let ourselves live in fear, especially because the spirit we get through Jesus is one of power, love, and a sound mind.

For God hath not given us the spirit of fear; but of power, and of love, and of a sound mind. (2 Tim. 1:7)

Understanding #4: He is My Supporter

Thou preparest a table before me in the presence of mine enemies: thou anointest my head with oil; my cup runneth over. (Ps. 23:5)

God spoke to David telling him to pen an inspirational and convincing message to His believers. The Father said, *let them know that they will be blessed to be prosperous over all their enemies. Tell them that they will be anointed with all I have to offer. Explain to them that they will have so much love, protection, knowledge, etc., that their cup (their lives) won't be able to contain it all!*

Being a worshiper of God gives us greener pastures than we could ever hope for. Putting our faith in God, praying to Him, praising Him, and letting Him take control of our problems leads us into a great positive. We will be led into greener pastures. Trusting in Him means that we don't have to fight our own battles. The Lord will do it for us, even the battles that are waged in our minds.

We demolish arguments and every pretension that sets itself up against the knowledge of God, and we take captive every thought to make it obedient to Christ. (2 Cor. 10:5 NIV)

If we can conquer the demons that are trying to get inside of our heads, we can conquer anything. The great thing is that God wants us to give Him power over this area of our lives. The battle you are fighting right now in life is a battle that is raging inside of your head. I know you may think that battle is with someone else. Maybe your battle is with some form of substance like drugs and alcohol. Initially, when a person starts using drugs, alcohol, or pornography, it is a "mind" problem—it begins as a moral decision in the mind. However, in time, what happens is that neurons that fire together when one engages in destructive behavior wire together. Eventually, an addict then moves from wanting to have drugs, alcohol, or pornography to having to have those things, so it *becomes a brain problem.* That explains why believers who become addicts find that even though they love Jesus, the Bible, and the church, they cannot break free. They need two things:

1) Other believers who will stand beside them and hold them accountable for their actions, and

2) A process that Paul calls "renewing the mind" found in Romans 12:2. The believer needs to saturate his mind with truth so that new pathways of neurons are created in his brain.

I'm here to tell you that the real battle starts within your mind. It's those thoughts that you cannot bring under control: the thought of anger could be what leads to a relationship breaking down, the thought that you "can't control that urge" could lead to substance abuse. Every battle you fight in life begins in the mind. So focus on this passage that Paul wrote about, *"bringing into captivity every thought" (2 Cor. 10:5),* then give that struggle to the Lord. When you conquer what's in your head, you can conquer any other situation.

Trust in God and give Him the work you need done. If you are willing to surrender everything over to the Lord, He will battle your demons no matter where they are—in your head, heart, or in the world. God will fight your battles.

> *And he said, Hearken ye, all Judah, and ye inhabitants of Jerusalem, and thou King Jehoshaphat, Thus saith the LORD unto you, Be not afraid nor dismayed by reason of*

this great multitude; for the battle is not yours, but God's. (2 Chron. 20:15)

Ye shall not need to fight in this battle: set yourselves, stand ye still, and see the salvation of the LORD with you, O Judah and Jerusalem: fear not, nor be dismayed; tomorrow go out against them: for the LORD will be with you. (2 Chron. 20:17)

Surely goodness and mercy shall follow me all the days of my life: and I will dwell in the house of the LORD forever. (Ps. 23:6)

God is the Protector against every enemy. You are not the one who needs to be out front in any of your battles. Let the Lord be your knight in shining armor. Pray to Him that He will come and save you from all, that He protects you from all.

CHAPTER 8

Your Weapon Against Toxicity

In the previous chapter I spoke to you about the need for prayer in your life to help you overcome everything toxic in your life. In this chapter I'd like to take it a bit further. Although praying is vital to having the Lord fight your battles, just as crucial to that defense is worship. The simple fact is that God wants you to worship Him.

The Hebrew word for "worship" is *Schachah,* which means "to worship, prostrate oneself, and bow down." In case you're not getting the point, to worship means to give honor to someone while physically laying yourself down. It's a physical act meant to show humbleness. It is the act of showing homage to someone more superior than you. David did it before Saul (1 Sam. 24:8). Ruth did it before Boaz (Ruth 2:10). Joseph saw a vision of all his brothers doing it before him (Gen. 37:5, 9-10). But the smartest people do it before God.

There was a certain disciple who threw himself down to the ground in worship when he realized the greatness of God.

> *But when Simon Peter saw it, he fell down at Jesus' knees, saying, "Depart from me, for I am a sinful man, O Lord." (Luke 5:8 ESV)*

Jesus Christ had just told Peter and his fishing crew to set out to deep waters and to let their nets down. Peter was hesitant. They had been fishing those waters all day long with no success. But because Jesus had asked him to do it, they did it. The resulting faith proved fruitful.

The result of that obedience was so richly rewarded with fish that the catch could well have sunk the boat because it was so abundant. Peter knew right away that this "man" before him was more than a typical man. He threw himself at Jesus' feet and told him, *"Depart from me, for I am a sinful man, O Lord" (Luke 5:8 ESV).*

Think about this situation for a moment. Fishermen were some of the gruffest and most austere people of that land. To have such a person thrust himself down prostrate before another was no meaningless thing. Peter had to be more than amazed. It must have been like seeing God himself! It was so awe-inspiring that a lifelong fisherman and fishing boat owner just up and left the only life he had ever known to follow that man. Most people, no matter how amazing an event might be, are not going to give up the profession that feeds their family. But Peter did. So did James and John of Zebedee. So did countless others. My point is that Peter's first thought when confronted with Jesus' power was to throw himself to the ground. That's some serious respect, the kind of respect we all must show the Lord.

Worshiping the Lord seems simple, doesn't it? Being a Christian doesn't have to be all that difficult. There aren't too many major rules to follow. In fact, the Book of Luke says to have faith in God and be saved in Luke 18:42. But isn't it smart to say that if you can't get the simple stuff right, then you shouldn't expect God to give you the deeper stuff? In this case the simple thing is this: If you want a defense against evil and the toxic things of this world, it helps to worship the Lord.

Worshiping God is a weapon against all the things attacking you. It's a plain and simple truth. There are some battles you fight where praise is the only weapon that will give you victory.

There are times when you quote the Word. There are times when you make positive affirmations. But there are also times you don't have the words to say. There are times when verses won't be there for you to quote. There are some battles so intense and so fierce that the only thing you can do is lift up your hands to the heavens and begin to worship.

I believe something happens when the devil sees that even in the midst of the battle, even in the midst of the disappointment, you are going to praise your Heavenly Father. And when you do, I picture the enemy dropping his head and saying a whole lot of words good Christian folk don't say. At that point the enemy knows his influence is abolished.

Remember that God will be praised whether we praise Him or not. Recall the time when Jesus came triumphantly riding into Jerusalem and the crowds began to shout and praise and honor Him?

> And when he was come nigh, even now at the descent of the mount of Olives, the whole multitude of the disciples began to rejoice and praise God with a loud voice for all the mighty works that they had seen ... (Luke 19:37)

The Pharisees quickly demanded that Jesus not only quiet His disciples from their outbursts of praise, but that He rebuke them for the praise they were offering Him. Listen to what He said,

> And he answered and said unto them, I tell you that, if these should hold their peace, the stones would immediately cry out. (Luke 19:40)

The very nature of God demands that He be praised and worshiped! If God's ultimate creation, mankind, refuses to give God the honor that is due Him, subordinate creation will cry out in praise and worship. Therefore, I believe it is important that we as the redeemed people of God bring glory to the One who has redeemed us and has miraculously written our names in the Lamb's Book of Life.

135

Understand that sanctification is not a "one and done" kind of thing. Through our faith our souls are redeemed once. Still, through our faith in Him we are sanctified daily. He delivers us from evil at every turn. He is the Redeemer (Ps. 19:14) not for just one moment but all moments. We must not simply ask for victory over a crucial moment or fear in our lives; we must claim victory over every aspect of our lives.

> *No, in all these things we are more than conquerors through him who loved us. (Rom. 8:37 NIV)*

If you expect to assert your authority over the things that oppress you, then you need to realize an indelible truth: You are not getting the victory—you already have it!

I hear many people say, "I am praying for a victory over the addiction I have in my life." While I understand what they are saying, I believe they are erroneous in their thinking. He doesn't say we <u>will become</u> more than conquerors; God's Word has declared that we are more than conquerors. When we get saved, we are positioned in heavenly places with Christ (Eph. 2:6). So because of our position in Him, we are victorious. We may go through difficult times in life, but that never takes away that in the midst of those difficult times, we are still victorious. In fact we can rest in the victory that even the difficult times of life will somehow work out for our good.

You are not fighting for your place in victory; you are fighting from a place of victory. And that position is far more superior than any spirit of offense, toxic relationship, or victim mentality that comes to poison your life. No matter what you're facing right now, you are more than a conqueror because of Christ. Act like the conqueror you are.

I never want to be guilty of not giving God the glory that's due Him. Just as I never want to misuse the blessings He's given me. Instead, I will praise Him each day and thank Him for all that I know I have and even what I'm unaware of that I have. Praise and worship exalt the Lord just as the Psalmist tells us they should.

> Let them exalt him also in the congregation of the people, and praise him in the assembly of the elders. (Ps. 107:32)

Not only does our worship exalt the Lord but also edifies the Body of Christ.

Something happens when we begin to worship God in the midst of any battle we are in. Something happens when our coworkers have turned spiteful against us for no reason or we feel that our family is backbiting against us—just when we think we are under an attack by a foe we cannot defeat, and we feel the pressure has grown to an insurmountable level. We may have talked to every one of our closest supporters but still don't know what to do. That something is the still whisper of God telling us that He has our backs.

Suddenly, we lift up our hands and begin to worship God. Suddenly, there comes a stream of His presence flowing through us. It causes us to see the evident answer, the answer that wasn't there a minute ago. Yet at the moment of worship, it comes rushing upon us. At that moment we understand that no foe is too strong for our faith and our God.

> . . . weeping may endure for a night, but joy cometh in the morning. (Ps. 30:5b)

Worship is our weapon against everything. That includes Satan, all his spirits, and all that is toxic in this world. Worship has become our tool for fighting all that's against us. It's what pierces through the clouds of doubt that encircles your mind. It's what will open up the way where there seems to be no way out.

Do not doubt your weapon. Doubt neither pleases the Lord nor causes us to grow.

But when you ask, you must believe and not doubt, because the one who doubts is like a wave of the sea, blown and tossed by the wind. That person should not expect to receive anything from the Lord. Such a person is double-minded and unstable in all they do. (James 1:6-8 NIV)

Doubt and fear are spiritual narcotics the devil uses against your faith. I believe that there are people who are literally addicted to fear and doubt. The moment God starts to do something great in their lives, that narcotic of doubt and fear kicks in. That mind-altering spiritual drug of doubt causes them to believe that they are incapable or unworthy to receive anything good from God. *Why should God bless me with a raise? Why should God bless me with an open door to ministry or business?* It gives God great pleasure to bless His children. So don't let the narcotics of doubt alter our faith. Rather, go into today knowing this: <u>Faith will</u> cancel out your doubt or <u>doubt will</u> cancel out your faith: you get to choose which one wins.

So how do worship, praise, and faith become our weapons against things like toxic people? The answer is it's a power we are given simply by declaring that God is our Father, and He is bequeathing His power to us. By admitting that God is the Highest—saying praises to Him—qualifies us for His protection against *anything!*

Worship and faith in God are not things that require a bunch of effort. Together they are a declaration of truth.

Know ye that the LORD he is God: it is he that hath made us, and not we ourselves; we are his people, and the sheep of his pasture. (Ps. 100:3)

Worship is not an emotion. It is also not something that can be worked up to make people feel good.

True spiritual worship happens when God's people recognize who God is. They recognize His preeminence and His providence. They begin to worship Him. True worship is never based simply on what God has done but who He is.

Think of it this way: Worship = Worth Ship.

It means the <u>state of worth</u>. It's based on the worthiness of God.

It's easy to worship the Lord when everything is going well and no one is attacking you, when no one is accusing you of anything, when you are not abusing any substances, and your relationships are intact. But the question is, can we keep feeling this good about things when it all goes awry? Can you still praise Him? Worship Him? In the midst of your storm?

Here's another point to ponder that will increase your ability to rebuke toxins. There's a difference between praise and worship.

We praise God for what He has done. We worship God for who He is. When we can get beyond just seeing God as the source for meeting our needs, get into the place where we begin to know Him for who He is, it will take our worship to an entirely different dimension.

When you can work through praising Him for His provisions, and you can work into worshipping Him for His person, then <u>worship has become your weapon</u>.

Developing this kind of weaponry means that almost nothing can poison your life.

Job understood this concept of worship being based on the person of God rather than his provision from God because when Satan had been allowed to attack Job and all that he possessed and loved, look at how Job responded:

At this, Job got up and tore his robe and shaved his head. Then he fell to the ground in worship and said: "Naked I came from my mother's womb, and naked I will depart. The LORD gave and the Lord has taken away; may the name of the LORD be praised." (Job 1:20-21 NIV)

He had a proper understanding of the character of God. Even though God didn't reveal Himself through provisions and prosperity, it took nothing away from who God was.

"But if I go to the east, he is not there; if I go to the west, I do not find him. When he is at work in the north, I do not see him; when he turns to the south, I catch no glimpse of him. But he knows the way that I take; when he has tested me, I will come forth as gold." (Job 23:8-10 NIV)

You might be wondering why God allows things to happen to you. Or you might wonder why the toxic things of this world are allowed to mess with you. Why does God's directing and protecting hand seem to disappear at times?

The clearest answer is that it doesn't.

Each of us have to comprehend that God's character is not based on our condition. Our condition is going to change because God, life, choices, and the devil keep on affecting things. But God's character never changes.

Jesus Christ the same yesterday, and to day, and for ever. (Heb. 13:8)

If the only time you worship God is when conditions are favorable and your needs are met, then your worship will be inconsistent, erratic, and unpredictable. How then would that be worship at all—real and loving worship, anyway?

140

Your worship must be based on the person of God. He is a person. A real person . . .

El Shaddai (Lord God Almighty)

El Elyon (The Most High God)

Jehovah Nissi (The Lord My Banner)

Jehovah Raah (The Lord My Shepherd)

Jehovah Shammah (The Lord Is There)

Jehovah Tsidkenu (The Lord Our Righteousness)

Jehovah Jireh (The Lord Will Provide)

Jehovah Shalom (The Lord Is Peace)

Jehovah Sabaoth (The Lord of Hosts)

So to worship Him only when you need something or when it's convenient means your relationship is dependent on your circumstances . . . meaning that it's not worship at all.

True worship is going to be based on the principles of the Word of God rather than the preferences of religion. Maybe tradition has taught you that there is no place for your lifting up your hands in worship. Yet the Word of God teaches differently.

> *I will therefore that men pray every where, lifting up holy*
> *hands, without wrath and doubting. (1 Tim. 2:8)*

Has tradition taught you that clapping your hands in church is not a welcome thing, when in fact, Scripture tells us to *"O clap your hands, all ye people" (Ps. 47:1)?*

Maybe tradition has taught you that there should be a sanctimonious silence within the house of God. Yet Truth teaches us,

Make a joyful noise unto the LORD, all ye lands. (Ps. 100:1)

O clap your hands, all ye people; shout unto God with the voice of triumph. (Ps. 47:1)

The purpose of worship is to show God that we revere, love, and honor Him. And when true worship takes place, God responds with many blessings. But the reward we want to focus on here and now is that worship brings comfort, encouragement, and strength against any opposition.

Comfort, comfort my people, says your God. (Isa. 40:1 NIV)

What then shall we say, brothers and sisters? When you come together, each of you has a hymn, or a word of instruction, a revelation, a tongue or an interpretation. Everything must be done so that the church may be built up. (1 Cor. 14:26 NIV)

Praise be to the God and Father of our Lord Jesus Christ, the Father of compassion and the God of all comfort, who comforts us in all our troubles, so that we can comfort those in any trouble with the comfort we ourselves receive from God. (2 Cor. 1:3-4 NIV)

Therefore encourage one another and build each other up, just as in fact you are doing. (1 Thess. 5:11 NIV)

Worshiping God is a weapon that sets us up to receive. We gain so much that our gain far surpasses God's. Perhaps the most valuable gift we gain through worship is that it opens the door to the presence of God. Being in His presence is protection. What evil can stand to be in front of God and survive? None.

As smoke is driven away, so drive them away: as wax melteth before the fire, so let the wicked perish at the presence of God. (Ps. 68:2)

Worship is one of the keys that unlocks the gates to God's presence and power. Anything that is going to be accomplished in your life is going to be accomplished through the presence and power of God. Human understanding, human enlightenment, human strength will never bring anything of spiritual significance to pass. It's because nothing is done by our hand. It is done only by the power of the Lord encouraged by our worship and faith.

Then he answered and spake unto me, saying, This is the word of the LORD unto Zerubbabel, saying, Not by might, nor by power, but by my spirit, saith the LORD of hosts. (Zech. 4:6)

That presence and that power of God will be brought about when you bring yourself into a state of spiritual worship. It was only after the people began to shout and the trumpets were blown that the walls of Jericho fell. God wanted His people to know that the power of God falls when praises to Him arise.

Never forget that God is our Provider, and His commission always includes His provision. He wants you to be protected. Seeing how He can do just that for you, you should faithfully ask for His favor. He is capable of keeping you safe from every sort of evil.

Faithful is he that calleth you, who also will do it. (1 Thess. 5:24)

God's commission for your life will always be accompanied by God's provision and power for you to do it. God wants you to succeed, especially against those things the enemy is trying to poison you with. Therefore, you can always be assured that whenever God calls you to do something, He will always provide what you need to do it. You don't have to depend on human strength or wisdom to achieve what God has called you to do. In fact, if you are depending on your strength, then maybe God didn't call you to do it.

His grace is all you need to achieve what you are supposed to do in life. So consider today what it is that you feel called to achieve but have never attempted. Is it because you fear you can't do it? Receive this word today; **God's provision will always follow God's commission.** You can do this when you start trusting in His grace to do it.

CHAPTER 9

How to Set Boundaries for Toxic People

Are you too busy? Is all of your energy spent on cases that will show no fruit? Are you trying to do too much for all the wrong people? Are your interests misplaced? If so, you are not doing what God wants you to do. He desires for you to be productive. In order to be efficient with people and their salvation, you must learn to use your time and energy the right way. Doing so requires setting boundaries and focusing on the right things at the right time.

She [Martha] had a sister called Mary, who sat at the Lord's feet listening to what he said. (Luke 10:39 NIV)

Are you busy doing all the wrong things like Martha? Do you find yourself running from one appointment to the next, answering emails and phone calls late into the evening, and wondering if you are ever going to get a break? It's almost funny when I hear people asking others how they are doing and allowing that dreadfully common response, "I'm just so busy!" I always wonder if their "business" is even productive.

I understand how life can get complicated and flat-out busy. We all get to that point in life that I call the "Martha Complex" where we neither set any boundaries for ourselves nor believe that we have the option to select what we do with the twenty-four hours we are given each day. So many people believe they have no choice in the matter that if there is a person who needs help or a task to be performed, it's their job to do it. That's just not the case. It's not "correct" for you to be so busy that you're living someone else's life.

Think about the two sisters in this Scripture—Martha and Mary. The story has Jesus visiting in their house. Jesus sits in a room, and it seems that every guest and all the residents of that house flock to the Lord to hear what He has to say.

Jesus is there to commune and teach. The Word said that the people there *"heard his word" (verse 39),* meaning that He was teaching. While He was teaching, Martha felt it was her obligation to serve the guests. She was probably making a meal and attending to her guests' needs. After all, she was the one who invited Jesus into her home. She probably believed it was her duty to work while Jesus taught.

Martha was doing everything herself while her sister Mary sat at Jesus' feet and listened. Martha became frustrated and went to Jesus. In a few words she asked the Lord why He didn't care about what she was doing. Why did He not tell her sister to help her serve? Jesus' response was something we all need to adopt into our lives.

Point blank, Jesus told Martha that she herself was the one who was wrong in the situation. He said that Mary had chosen the right thing by choosing to hear His teachings rather than go to work trying to comfort others.

Mary understood what was important to her, and Jesus commended her for it. It's amazing the strength and clarity you receive when you invest a few moments in the presence of Jesus. It's not like all the other things in your life will disappear; you'll simply have a better grasp on how to carry out your tasks and where to focus your efforts.

Mary was wise to make the choice she did. Whether she knew it, she was setting her boundaries. She chose to focus her efforts on the right thing. She could have run to help Martha with the food or other comforts for the guests, but instead she understood that she may never have this kind of chance again. Learning from a prophet of God in her own home was much more important than doing her part in helping guests.

Can you do what Mary did? Are you able to step away from helping others so you can ensure you make time to spend with Jesus? Do you have the power and wisdom to set appropriate boundaries? If not, you had better find out how to. Setting boundaries is crucial to your health and productivity, especially in regard to helping toxic people. The quicker we learn how to identify toxic people in our lives, the more time and energy we will save for the important people in our lives.

Throughout this book, we have focused on some vital information: Toxic Relationships, People with a Victim Mentality, People with a Manipulative Spirit, People with an Emotionally Abusive Personality, the Spirit of Offense, and more.

But what occurred to me is that many times we don't realize we are dealing with a toxic person until we are deep into the relationship. By that time we have wasted an enormous amount of time and energy trying to make something work with someone who more than likely will never go anywhere.

An unhealthy person will infect your life like toxins infect the human body. After some exposure, everyone around you starts to feel sick.

I'm an eternal optimist. I live on the high side of life and believe the best about people. The optimist in me hopes that toxic people will become better. And the good news is that some of them will with the right care and attention in a healthy environment. Unhealthy people can grow to become healthy, but I will say that it takes a tremendous amount of time and energy to see these people get to a place of emotional health.

But I've also come to the reality of this fact:

Some unhealthy people will not get better because they simply don't want to.

They remain difficult no matter how hard you try to work with them. They remain critical no matter how much you try to show them the positives of life. They remain bitter no matter how many words of healing you try to give to them. There are some toxic people who will live the rest of their lives with internal toxins because they choose to do so. You will never be able to help people heal until they are ready to be healed. They have to make the choice to get better. You will never be able to make that choice for them.

I get that there are people out there who want to do it all for some people. They are those who want to go down into the valley of toxicity and put such people on their back and carry them out. They can do this if they want to. But most likely those people will find their way back into that valley of toxicity needing to be rescued again.

You might be the kind of person who thinks it is your life mission to carry everyone on your back. You have this hero mentality where you feel like you are one of the characters in that superhero movie who's so popular, it's your job to save people from their own toxic demise.

You are not a superhero.

My flesh and my heart faileth: but God is the strength of my heart, and my portion for ever. (Ps. 73:26)

You are human. Too many times we get into "superhero" mode, thinking that we have to save everyone and fix everything.

That's wrong. The whole time we may be denying that there are things in our own lives that need to be fixed. These are emotions that you have repressed because you are trying to make everyone else happy, only to find that you have made yourself unhappy and vulnerable.

Today is the day to take off the cape and discover that you are a real human being with real emotions and genuine desires. Stop putting those emotions and desires on the shelf because you are too busy saving the day for everyone else. Start feeling those emotions you have repressed. Be human today! Do this by setting boundaries for yourself. Make yourself take time for you. Focus on you.

While your motives may be pure, the reality is that if you could help everyone, then you would be better than God Himself. Now I realize that Jesus repeatedly stated that none of His followers whom the Father had chosen, called, and justified would ever be lost. For example, in his high priestly prayer in John 17:12, Jesus prayed, *"I protected them [my disciples] and kept them safe by that name you gave me. None has been lost except the one doomed to destruction so that the Scripture would be fulfilled"(NIV).* In Romans 8:30 Paul states that **all** who are "called" are also "justified" and then "glorified." So the assumption is that all those that are "called" eventually become "glorified" and that glorification can't be lost. However, there are millions of people who, regardless of how much God tries to reach out (calls) to them with love and mercy, they still choose to die lost and go to hell. Believe me when I say that heaven is not a prison; if someone gets there and realizes that they don't like it, they can leave and go straight to hell. That's not being mean, that's a fact—just ask Lucifer and all of his little cronies.

Healing comes down to a personal choice that individuals make for themselves. No amount of counseling with them, crying with them, and pleading with them will ever change who they are or what they do until they are ready to change for themselves. So stop thinking that you must possess that hero mentality.

HOW TO SET BOUNDARIES FOR TOXIC PEOPLE

There are some of you reading this who have always been the counselor. You are the ones whom everyone reaches out to in times of hardship and despair. You are the shoulder that everyone cries upon, the one whose advice just seems to make everything better, the "Mr. or Mrs. Fix-it" who wrap themselves in the identity of "This is just who I am." Because of that, all of your time and energy have been wrapped up in trying to make everyone else better, leaving you and all of your issues on the shelf. You must think, "When I have more time, I'll take care of my own problems. At that time, maybe I'll better my prayer life or deal with my shortcomings." If that is you, then that day has come. It's called today.

Here is what I need to teach you in this chapter: you might be at the place where if you don't set some boundaries in your own life, you are going to burn out from lack of boundaries. I want to be careful here because I know that some of the people reading this will react overtly that I'm cautioning people against helping others. Some people might make the proclamation that we are here to give grace to everyone and help as many people as we can.

And when the woman saw that she was not hid, she came trembling, and falling down before him, she declared unto him before all the people for what cause she had touched him, and how she was healed immediately. (Luke 8:47-48)

Then touched he their eyes, saying, According to your faith be it unto you. (Matt. 9:29)

But listen, the only way to deal with toxic people who will drain you on every level is to learn to set healthy boundaries in your relationships with them. Creating healthy boundaries is empowering.

Boundaries are limits we set in order to . . .

Protect our own self-esteem

HOW TO SET BOUNDARIES FOR TOXIC PEOPLE

Maintain our own self-respect

And enjoy healthy and Godly relationships.

Let's start off with addressing self-esteem. Now I know that the term "self-esteem" does not appear in the pages of Scripture and that most contemporary Americans often struggle with self-esteem because of their own sinfulness. We who were created in God's image have become rebels against God. As C.S. Lewis said, "Fallen man is not simply an imperfect creature who needs improvement: he is a rebel who must lay down his arms."

But Scripture does speak of mankind in a fallen state as sinful and worthless. When Adam and Eve disobeyed God, the image of God in them was marred. For example: *"None is righteous, no, not one; no one understands; no one seeks for God. All have turned aside; together they have become worthless..."(Rom. 3:10-12a ESV).*

We cannot restore our own worth. Fallen, sinful man is incapable of approaching a holy, perfect God. For this reason, God, because of his great love for us, sent a mediator, his only-begotten Son Jesus Christ, to live a perfect life and die for our sins so that we might be reconciled to him. Christians are to determine their worth by believing what God has done for them in Christ and the new relationship that they have with God as his adopted children.

On the other side of the coin, we must understand that a lack of boundaries can cause emotional pain that can lead to despondency, depression, anxiety, and even stress-induced physical illness.

Having no boundaries is like leaving the front door to your home wide open where anyone—including uninvited guests—can enter in whenever they want. Personal boundaries are what define your identity. It's like the property lines around your house. This is my property and that is not my property. This is me, this is what I value, what I'm good at, what I believe, what I need and feel. This is not me, I don't believe those things, I don't need those things, I don't value those things; it's time to get away from me.

Now the first reaction that many of us will have is to question if it is selfish to set boundaries. We are followers of Christ, after all. Therefore, shouldn't we have the same compassion for people He did and have mercy on everyone? Shouldn't we be available for people whenever they need us just like Christ was available?

The answer is no! Our Lord was not available 24/7 when He was on this earth. He is now, but He wasn't when He was in the flesh. And just like Him, we need to have boundaries. Jesus set boundaries for Himself. He set boundaries around His personal needs. For example, He ate healthy food. He got the sleep he needed and even took naps. Jesus took time to relax, pray, and spend time with those who mattered most to Him.

> *But so much the more went there a fame abroad of him:*
> *and great multitudes came together to hear, and to be*
> *healed by him of their infirmities. (Luke 5:15-16)*

There are some of you who are being thronged by crowds. They are calling you and trying to get you to come over. You need to follow the example of Jesus and withdraw yourself. He withdrew from the crowds to go away on retreat, alone or with friends. He was never in a hurry, except to go to Jerusalem and embrace His cross.

Jesus set boundaries on inappropriate behavior. He fought his way through the crowd that was trying to throw Him off a cliff for claiming to be the Messiah.

> *All the people in the synagogue were furious when they*
> *heard this. They got up, drove him out of the town, and*
> *took him to the brow of the hill on which the town was*
> *built, in order to throw him off the cliff. But he walked right*

through the crowd and went on his way. (Luke 4:28-30 NIV)

Jesus set a boundary on entitlement. He didn't give in to His mother and brothers who tried to use their relationship with Him to pull Him away from the crowd He was ministering to.

While he yet talked to the people, behold, his mother and his brethren stood without, desiring to speak with him. Then one said unto him, Behold, thy mother and thy brethren stand without, desiring to speak with thee. But he answered and said unto him that told him, Who is my mother? and who are my brethren? And he stretched forth his hand toward his disciples, and said, Behold my mother and my brethren! For whosoever shall do the will of my Father which is in heaven, the same is my brother, and sister, and mother. (Matt. 12:46-50)

There are some people who think they are entitled to you. They get angry if you spend time with anyone else. That is a toxic relationship, and you are not helping them by yielding yourself to their every desire. These are the people who will call your phone many times in a row until you answer it. These are the people who believe that they are the only people on earth that matter and that all people should drop whatever they're doing to cater to their every desire. These are simple examples of toxic people, and today it's time for you to not only set basic limits that they may cross but also be extremely bold and to rid your life of them. That's not being harsh, just very honest.

Jesus set boundaries on baiting questions. When the religious leaders asked him baiting questions to make him look foolish, He answered with incisive questions of his own.

And when he was come into the temple, the chief priests and the elders of the people came unto him as he was teaching, and said, By what authority doest thou these things? and who gave thee this authority? And Jesus answered and said unto them, I also will ask you one thing, which if ye tell me, I in like wise will tell you by what authority I do these things. The baptism of John, whence was it? from heaven, or of men? And they reasoned with themselves, saying, If we shall say, From heaven; he will say unto us, Why did ye not then believe him? But if we shall say, Of men; we fear the people; for all hold John as a prophet. And they answered Jesus, and said, We cannot tell. And he said unto them, Neither tell I you by what authority I do these things. (Matt. 21:23-27)

There are some people who don't want answers. They just want to debate you. The reason I know that is they are ignoring the answer that you already gave them.

Jesus set a boundary on manipulation. There were times when even the Apostles of Jesus wanted Him to be something other than what He was sent to do. Do you remember when Jesus told them He came to die, but Peter did not want this to be so?

Then Peter took him, and began to rebuke him, saying, Be it far from thee, Lord: this shall not be unto thee. But he turned, and said unto Peter, Get thee behind me, Satan: thou art an offence unto me: for thou savourest not the things that be of God, but those that be of men. (Matt. 16:22-23)

Jesus set a boundary on his expectations for people in need. Two blind men called out to Him for help from the Jericho road.

> *And, behold, two blind men sitting by the way side, when they heard that Jesus passed by, cried out, saying, Have mercy on us, O Lord, thou son of David. And the multitude rebuked them, because they should hold their peace: but they cried the more, saying, Have mercy on us, O Lord, thou son of David. And Jesus stood still, and called them, and said, What will ye that I shall do unto you? (Matt. 20:30-32)*

They needed to ask for what they needed, and they needed to trust Him.

Toxic people are generally one of the following: they either want all of your assistance, or they are unwilling to admit they need any help at all from you or anyone else. Until they admit that they need help, they will never be healed. Jesus knew this. That's why He waited for the men to ask for help. He was not going to simply do everything for the men until they admitted that they needed Him. Then they told Him what they needed, and Jesus obliged. He set a boundary on what He would do.

The impotent man at the Sheep Gate lay there for thirty-eight years blaming other people for his inability to get into the pool so he could be healed. You know the man I'm speaking of? Look at how Jesus responded to him.

> *When Jesus saw him lying there and learned that he had been in this condition for a long time, he asked him, "Do you want to get well?"*

> *Then Jesus said to him, "Get up! Pick up your mat and walk." (John 5:6, 8)*

It was up to the man to be motivated and to take responsibility for himself. I could go on and on with how Jesus set boundaries for His own personal well-being but also boundaries around the people He dealt with.

HOW TO SET BOUNDARIES FOR TOXIC PEOPLE

The key to dealing effectively with toxic people is to learn the art of setting personal boundaries. It is not un-Christlike to set boundaries. It doesn't make you a bad person to set boundaries. It is for your own personal well-being to set boundaries.

Here are some key areas to protecting your life while using boundaries:

Boundary #1: Set a Boundary on Your Time

Teach us to number our days, that we may gain a heart of wisdom. (Ps. 90:12 NIV)

You are given only twenty-four hours every single day. When those twenty-four hours are gone, you will never get them back again. Every single person has the same amount of time. No one is given any more and no one is given any less, unless they die. What you do with those twenty-four hours is completely up to you as long as you know that the long-term results of your life will be determined by how you spend your time.

I tell you that because **toxic people don't care how much they infringe on your time.** What happens many times is that we find ourselves using the valuable time we have trying to talk to people who have no intention of changing. We come to the end of the day emotionally exhausted because our time has been spent on individuals who sap the energy from us rather than chasing the goals God has placed within us.

Time is a limited resource. But it's also your most valuable resource. I believe all of us feel as though we never have enough time to focus on what is most important in life. If you were to stop most people and ask how they are doing, most would say, "I am just so busy." But why are they so busy?

I believe it's because we have failed to protect the most valuable asset we have—the time we have been given.

Time is wasted on mindless conversations that don't benefit anyone. Time is wasted scrolling through people's complaints on social media. You allow friends and coworkers to make demands on your time to listen to their problems. You are doing tasks that you could easily have someone else do. Every moment spent on someone who is not willing to change is a moment that could be spent chasing your God-given goals in life. Therefore, I say quit wasting your time with people who don't add value to your life's purpose.

Boundary #2: Set a Boundary on Your Emotions

Keep thy heart with all diligence; for out of it are the issues of life. (Prov. 4:23)

The word "keep" means to guard with fidelity, to be kept close, be blocked. This is important to us because our emotions should be well-protected. Toxic people will say or do hurtful things, many times unintentionally. Still, that damages our emotions and our hearts. It hinders our ability to pour out the love of God for the people who need it most.

Too often we allow how others are feeling to affect our own emotions. Their sadness makes us feel sad. Their depression makes us feel depressed. Suddenly, we find ourselves sacrificing our own sense of happiness because of the emotions of other people. We need to protect our hearts and our emotions, especially against immature, irresponsible people.

Boundary #3: Set a Boundary on Your Energy

Just like time, you have only a certain amount of energy each day. Your energy is the wellspring from which you function. Most of us get that energy from time alone with God or activities that invigorate us. When we leave that alone time, we are ready to take on the world and be that soldier God needs. We will soar like eagles.

> *But they that wait upon the LORD shall renew their strength; they shall mount up with wings as eagles; they shall run, and not be weary; and they shall walk, and not faint. (Isa. 40:31)*

Toxic people have a way of draining your energy because they take away that time you need to recharge and reboot. They expect you to sit with them and focus your efforts in their direction rather than doing what you need to do for you and God. It's the spirit of toxicity that drives them to manipulate your efforts and use up your energy. The spirit of toxicity they possess drains the joy right out of you, and you become like a half-charged flashlight or cell phone battery.

One of the most hindering things that can happen to me is to have my cell phone lose its charge when I need it most. It's amazing how it seems to happen at the most inconvenient times. I'm just about to say something extremely important and it goes dead, leaving the person on the other end wondering what I was about to say.

Usually if our cell phone battery dies, it's because we didn't take the time to recharge the battery so we would be ready for a full day of usage. All it takes is a fully charged battery before heading into your day to avoid the issue. Yet I bet there has been at least one time each of us has done it.

Some of you are like *half-charged* cell phone batteries. Your spiritual and emotional batteries are charged only partially. Consequently, you die out at the most inopportune time of the day. It's because the toxic people in your life are draining you both emotionally and spiritually. You need to understand that the level of energy you possess is limited. If you don't recharge, you'll become ineffective and unhappy.

Boundary #4: Set a Boundary on Your Personal Values

Anything in your life that is important to you must have boundaries. My family is very important to me. That is why I have made it clear that I will never allow my ministry, business, or work to become more important than my family. Too many Christian leaders have lost their children because the church became more important than their children.

Do not allow the toxic emotions of people to change your personal set of values. Respect yourself enough to stand firm on what you believe and who you are. Don't sacrifice your dreams for the sake of pleasing others.

Believe me when I say that the spirit of offense and other toxic spirits will attach themselves to the people you have around you in order to try to get you to change. These toxic spirits will do anything they can to break your boundaries. If they can't get to you directly, they'll come indirectly. Never settle when it comes to your values.

CHAPTER 10

Conclusion

The world is getting kind of crazy. People are losing control over themselves, losing their way to the devil. And this seems to be happening at an alarming rate. With your understanding of this truth, you should have no problem realizing that it is past time to take a stand against all manner of evil.

The toxicity of our world brought about by Satan aims to ruin our world and destroy our hopes of salvation through Jesus Christ. Of course Satan can't overturn the will and purpose of our God Almighty regarding his salvific work in the lives of the people whom he has chosen, but Satan still tries to implant deception, lies, and confusion into our minds causing us to doubt in Whom we've believed and trusted for salvation. He utilizes the following major components in his arsenal: toxic spirits, toxic relationships, and toxic substances to poison our relationships. This includes all of our relationships—those with one another and with God. We must not allow evil to overcome our good.

Throughout this book I've spoken to you about realizing what's around you and have also explained how you might achieve positive change in your life. You've seen examples of toxicity. You've learned that it is everywhere or at least that it can be. It can be found within the lives of our closest friends and family. And it is there in the lives of strangers. You have seen examples of how a spirit that attaches itself to an offense differs from a manipulative and domineering spirit. You should have learned how to pinpoint toxic relationships and even how not to be offended.

Through it all I want you to understand some truth: that **all** toxicity is absorbed into our lives through people. People are the source that brings anything destructive into our lives. Therefore, I'll leave you with two helpful hints aimed at reducing the toxicity in your life.

Hint #1: Love People

The Beatles sang it and Jesus said it: All you need is love. Our Lord told us to love our neighbors *(Matt. 22:29)*, love our enemies *(Matt. 5:44)*, and love ourselves *(Mark 12:33)*. It is crucial to observe that there are *two* commands in Mark 12:33, *not three*: 1) Love God and 2) Love your neighbor. You **do love** yourself already. Every person makes choices to care for himself. Paul affirmed this truth in Ephesians 5:29 when he wrote *". . . no one ever hated his own body, but he feeds and cares for it . . ."*

Because we humans do this *automatically*, Jesus could command, Love your neighbor as yourself (because you already do that). You may not *like* yourself at times, but you make choices—an act of your own free will—that you think are the best for you. That is what Jesus commands you to do for your neighbor: make choices to do good deeds or actions for him or her as you already do for yourself.

The Greek word in Mark 12:33, *agapao*, does <u>not</u> mean "like"; it is not a word dealing with feelings or emotion; it is the Greek word for "love of the will." It is the word that Jesus used when he commanded his followers to "love" their enemies. Jesus did not command us to "like" them (to have warm fuzzy feelings), but as an act of the will to choose to do them good. It is the word that Paul used when he commanded husbands to "love" their wives *(Eph. 5:25)*. Even if things change in the marriage so that the wife is no longer "liked," the husband is commanded to treat her in such a way that he chooses to do good to her at all times. It is the universal power that can overcome any evil. It is a response that can fix many things around us.

> *And this is his commandment, That we should believe on the name of his Son Jesus Christ, and love one another, as he gave us commandment. (1 John 3:23)*

I love how John wrote to us that this is his "commandment" that we love one another. It's not a suggestion or an option. It's a commandment. There is a divine expectation for us to demonstrate to each other the same love that Jesus has demonstrated to us. How did He demonstrate that love? By laying down His life at Calvary so we could be saved. John 15:13 tells us,

> *Greater love hath no man than this, that a man lay down his life for his friends. (John 15:13)*

So if we are commanded to love as Jesus loves… what does that mean? It simply means that love is laying down your own agenda for the good of another person. It simply means that you are more concerned about their well-being than your own. In a world that is myopic and full of self-centered marketing and attitudes, true love focuses on the other person rather than yourself. True love asks what can I do for you? rather than demands what can you do for me? True love sacrifices what it wants so that you get what you need.

Jesus commanded that we love one another. It wasn't an option. So let's start loving Jesus and others to expel all the toxicity in this world.

Hint #2: Be Diligent

Working with people is super difficult. It requires the patience of a saint. So I'm telling you that you are going to get frustrated with people. You are going to want to stop trying to help them and focus solely on yourself. *Don't*. Be balanced, but also be diligent in your pursuit to force toxicity out of your life.

The Lord blesses you with a task, and He will also give you a diligent spirit to do that work. You simply need to have faith that God gave it to you.

> *Therefore, my brothers and sisters, make every effort to confirm your calling and election. For if you do these things, you will never stumble . . . (2 Pet. 1:10 NIV)*

The behavior of the people to whom Peter was writing left Peter in doubt of their salvation. He was exhorting them to provide evidence to themselves that they were really true believers—to make their calling and election verifiable by their behavior. Compare *Hebrews 12:14: "Strive for peace with everyone, and for the holiness without which no one will see the Lord."*

God always treats people as moral agents; what may be absolutely certain in God's mind from his eternal purpose is that it "shall" be so. However, this can be made certain **to us** only by evidence, in the free exercise of our own wills.

The meaning here is clear: they were to seek such evidence of personal holiness as to put the question of whether they were "called" and "chosen"—so far as their own minds were concerned—to rest; in other words, they were urged to provide undoubted evidence on this point.

Your motivation IS: God will not forsake you, so be diligent to do good *(Heb. 13:5)*. He is going to give you everything you need to complete the mission that He's set before you. After all, when you are doing His work, why wouldn't He?

Now go out there and make your life and this world a less toxic place!

Made in the USA
Middletown, DE
28 October 2022

13599084R00104